The Classroom Teacher's Guide to Supporting English Language Learners

This book answers your key questions about educating English Language Learners (ELLs) and offers detailed guidance and concrete applications for your classroom. Designed as a one-stop-shop for classroom teachers of all grade levels and content areas, this book is chock full of essential information, delivered in a practical, concise format. In each chapter, you will find checklists, instructional strategies, tables, tools and ideas for next steps. The resources and examples provided are easy to implement and can be used the next day in your teaching.

Topics addressed include:

- Getting to know your ELLs
- Considering how culture, language and academic background impact learning
- Bridging the home/school connection
- Pairing content and language objectives
- Gauging learner progress
- Collaborating with ELL staff
- Much more!

Pamela Mesta has been in the education field for over 20 years. She currently works as the Supervisor of ESOL in a large public school system in Maryland.

Olga Reber has been in education for 15 years. She currently works as an ESOL Resource Teacher in a large public school system in Maryland.

The Classroom Teacher's Guide to Supporting English Language Learners

Pamela Mesta and Olga Reber

Routledge
Taylor & Francis Group

NEW YORK AND LONDON

First published 2019
by Routledge
52 Vanderbilt Avenue, New York, NY 10017

and by Routledge
2 Park Square, Milton Park, Abingdon, Oxon, OX14 4RN

Routledge is an imprint of the Taylor & Francis Group, an informa business

Library of Congress Cataloging-in-Publication Data
Names: Mesta, Pamela, author. | Reber, Olga, author.
Title: The classroom teacher's guide to supporting English language
    learners / Pamela Mesta and Olga Reber.
Description: New York : Routledge, 2019.
Identifiers: LCCN 2019000765 (print) | LCCN 2019011456 (ebook) |
    ISBN 9781315819747 (ebook) | ISBN 9780415734769 (hbk) |
    ISBN 9780415733458 (pbk) | ISBN 9781315819747 (ebk)
Subjects: LCSH: English language—Study and teaching—Foreign
    speakers. | Limited English proficient students—United States. |
    Language arts—Correlation with content subjects—United States. |
    Learning disabilities—United States.
Classification: LCC PE1128.A2 (ebook) | LCC PE1128.A2 M277 2019
    (print) | DDC 428.0071—dc23
LC record available at https://lccn.loc.gov/2019000765

ISBN: 978-0-415-73476-9 (hbk)
ISBN: 978-0-415-73345-8 (pbk)
ISBN: 978-1-315-81974-7 (ebk)

Typeset in Palatino
by Swales & Willis Ltd, Exeter, Devon, UK

Contents

Preface

Our purpose in creating this book is simple . . . design a one-stop-shop for classroom teachers of all grade levels and content areas who are seeking to better support the English Language Learners (ELLs) in their classrooms. This book is chock full of essential information you need, delivered in a practical, concise, easy to read format. In each chapter, you will find checklists, instructional strategies, tables, tools and ideas for next steps. The resources and examples provided are easy to implement and can be used the next day in your teaching.

In Part I, we begin with important considerations for getting to know your ELLs. We'll take an in-depth look at how culture, language and academic background come together to impact learning. We will examine major linguistic challenges that an ELL faces and share ideas for addressing them in your classroom. Cultural differences will also be explored, and how these differences can easily lead to miscommunication and/or create unintentional barriers to learning. Practical ideas for connecting with families will also be shared.

In Part II of the book, we will delve into instruction and assessment. Our goal for this section is to provide pointed answers to major questions classroom teachers have, and offer detailed guidance and concrete applications across grade levels and subjects. Tips for pairing content and language objectives will be shared, along with guidance for lesson planning and modifying content and assessment. We'll spend considerable time on vocabulary instruction, and share inexpensive, easy-to-create activities and games that focus on introducing and strengthening academic language. Strategies for collaborating with ELL staff will be outlined. We'll also take a closer look at how to gauge learner progress, and steps you can take if you suspect there are issues beyond language.

Thanks for taking this journey with us! Happy reading!

About the Authors

Pamela Mesta has been in the education field for over 20 years. Her teaching and administrative experiences span all grade levels, and include English for Speakers of Other Languages (ESOL), early childhood/elementary education, teacher/program supervision and professional development. She currently works as the Supervisor of ESOL in a large public school system in Maryland.

Ms. Mesta holds a B.A. in Communication and a Master's degree in Education. Her post-graduate coursework includes educational leadership, ESOL, cultural proficiency and educational technology. She has also been an adjunct college professor for over 10 years. Professional highlights include building a model ESOL Program from the bottom-up, achieving National Board Certification, serving on numerous state and national ELL and education committees and being selected as a state level master teacher. She is also an experienced community and school interpreter/translator, and continues to provide training in that area. Ms. Mesta is especially passionate about providing practical, hands-on professional development and support for teachers, and regularly conducts training and workshops at the local, state and national levels on a variety of education-related topics.

Olga Reber has been in education for 15 years. Her teaching experience includes ESOL, English as a Foreign Language (EFL) and professional development. She currently works as an ESOL Resource Teacher in a large public school system in Maryland.

Mrs. Reber completed her schooling in Russia before moving to the U.S. She holds a B.S. in Secondary Education/Foreign Language Instruction and an M.A. degree in Linguistics. Her post-graduate coursework includes ESOL and educational technology. She has also been an adjunct college professor for close to 10 years. Professional highlights include serving on state ELL committees, being selected as a state level master teacher and co-presenting teacher workshops at the state and national levels. She is also an experienced community and school interpreter/translator, and continues to provide training in that area. Mrs. Reber is passionate about serving ELLs and continues to advocate for the students with whom she works.

Part I

Where to Start – Getting to Know Your ELLs

1

Who Are the ELLs in My Classroom?

Main Points

- ◆ Before creating an instructional plan for your ELLs, information about students' background and prior schooling needs to be gathered.
- ◆ Know what languages your students speak, and research characteristics of each.
- ◆ Not all students who come from the same language background and/or country will experience the same successes and difficulties.
- ◆ Take the time to consider and address cultural differences.
- ◆ Culture shock and trauma are significant factors that may influence language acquisition and academic progress.

Getting Started

"Where do I begin?" You may be asking yourself this question right now. Knowing where to start and what questions need answering about your ELLs can provide you with a great beginning point. In this chapter, we will explore how students' backgrounds, native languages and cultures impact learning.

There are *five key questions* to research about your ELLs:

1. What was his/her prior schooling like?
2. What is his/her native language (L1), and is he/she literate in that language?

Table 1.1 ELL Checklist

| Student name: | |
Date:	
Prior school experience(s):	
Native language (L1):	
L1 literacy level:	
Structure of L1/possible language transfer issues:	
English proficiency level/date of last assessment:	
Cultural differences/considerations:	

3. How is the L1 structured, and what does this mean as the student learns English?
4. What is their English level?
5. How will culture affect learning?

You can quickly capture the answers to these five questions in Table 1.1.

1. **What was his/her prior schooling like?** Details about a student's prior schooling will provide you with unique insight about his/her experiences as a learner, their content exposure and what schooling was like in his/her country. You may also discover strengths, weaknesses, interests and any academic concerns that may be present. It is also important to find out what value the family places on education, and what short- and long-term educational and career goals the family and the student share. Knowing your learners will help you choose the best tools and strategies for successful teaching and learning.

2. **What is his/her native language (L1), and is he/she literate in that language?** This is arguably the most important information you can find out about a student. L1 testing *(specifically in reading, writing and math)* can provide useful information, especially if a student has registered mid-year or if appropriate grade and level placement is in question.

   Students who are literate in their first language will be able to make deeper content and linguistic connections as they learn English. Think of it like having money in your bank account. The more you have, the more you can do . . . the same is true of having a strong command of your L1. A literate student understands that language is a system, with rules and exceptions to those rules. For example, a Spanish speaker knows that adjectives come directly after the noun they describe *(ex: "Tengo una camisa azul"* literal translation into English is: *"I have a shirt blue").* In this example, when the native Spanish speaker attempts to construct this sentence in English, he/she will most likely make the mistake of placing the adjective after the noun, since that is how the language is structured. If the student is literate in the L1, he/she will understand the teacher's explanation that adjectives precede nouns in the English language, as this explanation will make sense to a learner with a good language sense/understanding. An illiterate or a younger student, however, will have no point of reference, no knowledge base of parts of speech and, consequently, will have a more difficult time with concepts such as these.

3. **How is the L1 structured, and what does this mean as the student learns English?** A common misconception exists that in order to be an effective teacher of ELLs, you need to be able to speak your students' native language(s). *This is not so.* There is benefit, however, to knowing *characteristics* of the students' languages. Learning what sounds don't exist in the student's L1 compared to English, and what the word order of declarative and interrogative sentences looks like, for example, will help you anticipate difficulties students may encounter when learning English.

   When a person is learning a second language, it is natural for him/her to make comparisons to the L1. The learner will compare sounds, vocabulary and grammatical structures of the new language to his/her native language. *Language transfer* is the process of applying knowledge from the native language to the learning of a second language. Language transfer can be positive or negative.

   Positive language transfer refers to aspects of the L1 and L2 that are similar, and will be helpful when acquiring the new language. Some examples of positive language transfer include similar

Table 1.2 Negative Language Transfer Examples: English and Russian

English	Russian
Articles (a, an, the)	No articles used; Russian speakers will omit or misuse articles in English
Short and long vowels (sit – seat)	Short and long vowels are not differentiated; Russian speakers have a difficult time hearing the difference, consequently affecting pronunciation
/w/ and th /ɵ,ð/ sounds	Not present; difficult to produce when speaking English, these sounds often get replaced with /v/, /s/, /z/
Continuous and perfect tenses (*I listen. I am listening. I have listened.*)	No continuous or perfect tense; only one present, one past and one future tense exists
Countable and uncountable nouns	Countable and uncountable nouns exist but do not coincide with English (ex: *hair* in Russian is countable – *I brush my hairs every morning* – this would be a negative language transfer mistake

(or same) alphabet systems and sounds, as well as the presence of cognates *(words that share a common root/origin)*. We will explore cognates and other special linguistic considerations in Chapter 2.

Negative language transfer involves aspects of the native language that are significantly different from the second language. Negative language transfer examples include English sounds not present in the student's L1, false cognates *(words that look or sound the same in different languages but do not have the same meaning)* and, most importantly, grammatical structures of the English language that are significantly different from the student's L1. Knowing which negative transfer issues exist between English and a student's L1 will help you to plan specific language objectives you can pair with content objectives. Table 1.2 examines some of the differences between English and Russian.

When the ELL specialist and the classroom teacher look at the list above contrasting the features of the English and Russian languages, predictions can be made about possible negative language transfer issues. Instructional activities and lessons can be planned to target these particular difficulties. It is important to note, however, that not every speaker of the Russian language will experience the same difficulties and make the same language errors when learning English. For an additional example, Table 1.3 shows some contrasting features between English and Vietnamese.

Table 1.3 Negative Language Transfer Examples: English and Vietnamese

English	Vietnamese
Nouns receive plural marker -s	No plural marker used *"I have three sister."*
Present, past, and future tenses	Verb does not change to signify past tense *"I go to school yesterday."*
Verb "be" (He <u>is</u> hungry.)	"Be" is implied in the adjective form *"He hungry."*

Many resources exist that highlight in-depth transfer issues for various languages as compared to English. One of the most valuable things you can do is to ***study language transfer issues*** that affect your students. Help students to identify transferrable skills *(positive language transfer)* and reinforce the non-transferrable skills with specifically designed language exercises targeting these differences. Utilize charts such as Tables 1.2 and 1.3 to help guide your planning and instruction based on what you have learned about the student's linguistic background.

4. **What is their English level?** Consult with your ELL specialist to find out more about testing that has been completed on your students or request testing for students who may have been missed during the registration process. When testing students for English proficiency, ELL specialists generally assess four essential language domains *(listening, speaking, reading, writing)*. An overall score is usually given, with further breakdown into these language domains. Students may score high in some areas and low in others, depending on their prior schooling and exposure to English.

    Depending on the country, ELLs arrive with various experiences in English. Some have had English as a Foreign Language *(EFL)* instruction in their native country *(focusing on social language)* while others have not. If a student has had no prior exposure to English, they will score low in all language domains. It is important to note that students' skills in reading, writing, listening and speaking are generally not balanced. Knowing your students' language proficiency levels by domain will help to guide your instruction. For example, if you have a student with stronger listening and speaking skills, you may want to assess that student orally, or at least read directions aloud. That way there will be less of a language barrier when assessing content.

5. **How will culture affect learning?** Aside from the content and linguistic difficulties ELLs face, students also experience cultural challenges and culture shock as they transition to school in the United States. These differences often have a huge impact on learning. Being aware that such differences exist will help guide your instruction.

Attitudes Towards Education and Gender

Various cultures have very different views on education. In some cultures, families have higher expectations of males vs. females. This can influence a student's motivation and performance at school. Female students from cultures such as this can either show low interest in education or become torn between their traditional role in the family and the contrasting lives of their female peers from the United States. This, in turn, can affect behavior and academic performance.

Parent Involvement in Education/School Decisions

There are some countries where it is not appropriate for parents to interfere or question the teacher's decisions. Parents from cultures such as this will most likely avoid attending back-to-school nights or conferences, as they may not see themselves as a critical part of their child's education. The belief may be that education is the responsibility of the school and discipline is the responsibility of the parents. In addition, parents may feel uncomfortable when they are asked for their opinion about educational decisions such as course selection or grade placement.

Male/Female Participation and Expectations

This cultural difference has a lot to do with special areas instruction. In many countries, students are divided according to gender for physical education, technology and family/consumer sciences. Females coming from these societies may feel uncomfortable being placed in co-ed learning and social situations. At the same time, males may feel humiliated if they are expected to learn things like food and cooking. Understanding these differences will help educators to gain insight into students' atypical behaviors or initial refusal to participate in certain activities.

Higher level classes may only be offered for males in some countries where females aren't expected to be college or career ready. When students from such cultures enter a U.S. school and realize that none of the classes or activities are gender-specific, they may feel either embarrassed to participate *(if it's something that only the opposite gender traditionally does in their culture)* or not worthy and shy of being in a class that they believe is for the opposite gender only. An example of this would be a male ELL refusing to jump rope for warm-ups in physical education class because this was something only girls did in his country. Another example is when female students and their families feel uncomfortable about enrolling into an honor's math course because, culturally, females may not be expected to do so.

School Appropriate Clothing/Behavior

School appropriate clothing is a hot topic with all students, not just ELLs. However, clothing is also very cultural. There are some cultures where it is appropriate to wear more revealing clothes than considered acceptable in the United States. School behavior that is considered appropriate may also differ from culture to culture. Making eye contact with teachers or students of the opposite gender may not be the norm for some students. Or, talking with peers may not be allowed during instructional time, so group or collaborative activities may be confusing to students until they realize this is acceptable and encouraged.

Classroom Setting: Use of Visuals, Manipulatives and Hands-on Activities

In many countries, the only instructional materials used in class are textbooks, pencils and notebooks. Coming into an American school with bright posters and visuals on the walls, colorful manipulatives and project supplies (*sticky notes, highlighters, mechanical pencils*) as well as instructional technology may be a shocking and overwhelming experience to an ELL. Students might focus on their environment rather than the actual instruction until they get acclimated to their surroundings and feel comfortable, safe and competent.

School Age

Children may start school at age 4 or 5, or they may start school at 7 or 8, depending on the country. They may also be expected to graduate at a different age than is the norm in the U.S. These differences make it confusing for ELL families when they first move to the United States. It may appear to the families that their children are being unfairly placed behind a grade or two or accelerated too soon. Age-appropriate placement of ELLs arriving from other countries should always be the goal.

Content Covered in School

Although variances in curriculum exist state to state, generally the subjects covered in Pre-K-12 will look similar throughout public schools in the United States. However, students who come from other countries may have experienced ways and approaches to content that are quite different. For example, some countries do not cover male/female anatomy and reproduction in schools, because this matter is considered very private. Consequently, students from these countries may feel very uncomfortable when such topics are brought up. Another example about differences in content covered is in math. Some ELLs come with very strong computation skills but have never had the opportunity to solve a word problem applying those skills. Upper elementary students may know how to multiply double digit numbers in their head but may have never seen a fraction. These curricular differences across the world may give a false impression about a student's true level and general academic and cognitive ability.

Daily Routines

School buses, strictly enforced classroom and hallway rules, rigid bell schedules, a 30-minute lunch, assemblies and fire and tornado drills can make some ELLs feel anywhere from a little uncomfortable to extremely scared during their first few weeks in a new school. Take some time to ask the student what his/her prior daily routine was like. This will provide you with valuable information and help you to avoid potentially upsetting situations. This can be done with the help of an interpreter if needed. However, if the student has some English skills, and it is appropriate for your content, you can turn it into a project comparing their previous school with the new one. You will be surprised by the things you will both learn!

Cafeteria Food and Procedures

Some common U.S. foods may be so strange or aromatic to newcomers that they cannot get themselves to try them in the school cafeteria. Some ELLs explain that pizza has an offensive smell to them, and that peanut butter looks and tastes strange. Other times, the issue is not the food itself, but rather the process of getting it on the tray in the cafeteria, which causes confusion for some students. Many ELLs report being puzzled the first few weeks about which items are to be asked for (*and how to ask for them*), and how much/ many of each item is ok to place on their tray. Let's take a minute to see how this might play out in the cafeteria line. Imagine you are a newcomer and saw that there was a tray of cookies. You took two, not realizing there was a one cookie rule. An agitated cafeteria worker raises her voice at you, grabs both cookies off your tray and explains the rule. As a newcomer with limited English, these words and phrases are just a mess of sounds to you. All you can understand is "No . . . No . . . No." Would you want to go back to the cafeteria the next day? Probably not. *This situation could be avoided by accompanying your ELLs to the cafeteria, and having a proactive conversation with the cafeteria attendant.* Also consider assigning a peer buddy to new ELLs during their first week of school. This will help to alleviate the stress of uncertainty, as well as provide an opportunity for them to make new friends.

Hallway Behavior/Moving Between Classes

From Pre-K-12, students are expected to move around the school to reach their destination in a particular way or fashion. Either walking in a line following the teacher in elementary school or walking independently from class to class in high school, following school rules may be a new notion to many ELLs. Fire and tornado drills often prove to be scary and confusing to ELLs. Take some time to explain what these drills are and the procedures for each. In some cases it is beneficial to involve an interpreter to communicate this information, especially if the student comes from a war-torn country or a place with many natural disasters. For middle and high school level students, not being allowed to leave the school building during the day may be a new experience. In many countries students are allowed to go home for lunch. Asking the teacher to leave the class to use the restroom is another notion that needs to be explained to ELLs on their first day. To avoid misunderstandings or embarrassments that may stem from students' lack of cultural knowledge, a *proactive solution* is to schedule an interpreter to accompany the student and their family on a school tour where rules and procedures are explained and modeled.

Grading

This is one of the most common cultural differences. Students may come from a country where numbers are used for grading *(either a scale of 1–5 or 1–10)*, or a class ranking system *(1st, 7th, 21st in class)*. Upon registration, the ELL specialist/office should be consulted when evaluating transcripts and assigning credits and grades from other countries. School records from abroad, even when translated, do not easily compare to the U.S. system of grading. Class descriptions, their duration and frequency in a student's schedule, as well as grades earned may be difficult to decipher. Multiple resources are published that compare education systems across the world. Before deciding on a grade placement or creating a schedule for a middle or high school student, it is important to first evaluate the transcripts.

Another important grading issue to address is your ELL's understanding of the U.S. grading system. Take the time to explain your grading system prior to grading his/her first assignment. Another issue related to grading is cheating and/or plagiarism. In some countries, especially the ones with collective societies, it is not uncommon to receive and give help on tests and quizzes. These behaviors are not encouraged, but, at the same time, they are not punished. Students from these school systems are usually shocked to get a zero on an assignment just for looking at a classmate's paper. A conversation about individual work, cheating and plagiarism is also a necessary one to have with newcomers.

Methods of Testing/Assessment

In a typical American classroom, the majority of assessments are in written form. This may not allow students with stronger speaking and listening skills to show what they know. In many countries, schools hold oral exams with small writing components. Multiple choice tests are also rarely used. ELLs often struggle with test format. We will explore assessment further in Chapter 4. Table 1.4 contains a checklist of items to address which may serve as a guide to an ELL's introduction to a new school.

Addressing these cultural topics with students and their families from the beginning will prevent unnecessarily embarrassing moments and misunderstandings. It's important to remember that this will not prevent your ELL from encountering another cultural issue that may puzzle or confuse him/her. There is no way of knowing a complete list of what may be

Table 1.4 New Arrival Checklist

Student name: Date:	
Points to address	**Notes**
Cafeteria	
Hallway behavior	
Restrooms/water fountains	
Grading system	
Cheating/plagiarism	
Male/female participation expectations	
Schedule/daily routines	
Other	

drastically different between the U.S. and the culture of the ELLs in your classroom. It is also crucial to remember that if one of your ELLs exhibits a cultural difference, another student from a similar cultural background/ country may or may not present with the same difficulty or issue.

Culture Shock

If you have ever traveled abroad, you may have experienced *culture shock*. This is a term used to describe the feelings people have when they visit or move to an unfamiliar culture/location.

Immigrant and adopted children may experience culture shock and become withdrawn, passive or even aggressive. *The more differences there are between the new culture and their own, the greater the shock.* Some students have left behind grandparents or other relatives, friends, teachers and loved ones. Customs and traditions, as well as holidays, are also different. In the case of adopted children, they may still be adapting to the new family and surroundings. Even though they have an advantage of hearing the English language at home and expanding their vocabulary faster, they often do not have the opportunity to go home and speak their native language with families and siblings. Being immersed in an unfamiliar language and culture can make a person feel physically ill. He/she may experience severe headaches and nausea. That's why it is natural and healthy to want to speak your native language for a period of time throughout the day, or "shut down" and stop trying to process information completely. Teachers can alleviate this by allowing breaks for newcomers instead of trying to pack their day full of activities, assignments and worksheets.

Stage 1: Fascination

During this stage, students are excited about their new lives and opportunities. Everything is great, and they are enjoying learning about their school, meeting new friends and doing other new things. Students will also experience a "silent period" during this stage, which may last a few days or even a few months. This is a time when students are able to understand more than they are able to produce.

Stage 2: Adjustment

During this stage, the differences between the new culture and the native culture become more apparent and somewhat uncomfortable. Students may become increasingly tired and frustrated with the new surroundings and the new language. They realize that the new life is proving to be more challenging than they imagined it in the fascination stage. Signs of experiencing the adjustment phase may include aggression, irritability, work avoidance, distractibility or even depression. Students in this stage of culture shock need time and patience from their teachers.

Stage 3: Disenchantment

During this stage, students begin to deal with the challenges and differences between cultures and languages. They often miss their friends and relatives that were left behind, as well as familiar routines. Things may become too much for them to handle. There is confusion between old and new rules and traditions/beliefs. There are a lot of unanswered questions that students keep inside due to shyness or language limitations. Students begin to find coping mechanisms that are not always positive. Acting out can also happen in this stage. Sometimes parents become alarmed with this behavior. However, once students find support in a teacher or understanding in a new friend, they become more open to asking questions and trying new things. This may lead him/her back into the fascination stage.

Remember that culture shock is a cycle and ELLs will go through this several times before they adjust to new routines and start feeling comfortable in your classroom. Once a student fully acculturates, or adapts to the new culture, they feel safe and prosper. They begin to accept both cultures and languages. Students begin to adopt the mainstream culture at school but may still continue to follow the values of the home culture outside of school.

Making relationships with your ELLs is essential. New students benefit greatly from having a trusting relationship with a teacher, a counselor or an administrator. It takes time to develop such a relationship, especially with students who have experienced trauma in their lives. School rules, routines, consequences, as well as some classroom expectations may become triggers of negative memories or traumatic experiences. Many things in a new country and school are difficult to understand and very easy to misinterpret due to cultural differences and language barriers. It is not unusual for educators who work closely with ELLs to hear heartbreaking stories that students choose to share with them orally or in their writing. Some of the experiences are so violent that they will affect the child for the rest of his/her life. It is important to be sensitive to this when working with ELLs.

Reflection Questions

1. Choose a language to compare with English. Fill in the chart below comparing the features of both languages. For example, if you choose Spanish, the similarity can be the alphabet. One of the differences you can point out is the use of adjectives before the

nouns they describe in English (*the orange cat*) while in Spanish the adjective comes after the noun it describes (*the cat orange*). Where would you start your English instruction: with the similarities or the differences? Why?

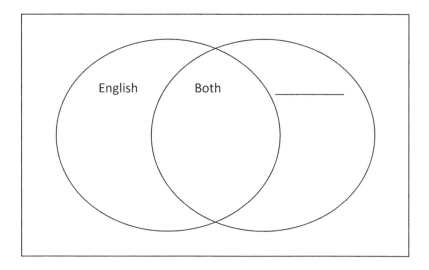

2. Think of a cultural aspect from the U.S. that could cause confusion or misunderstanding to students/parents from other countries. How might you introduce/address it?
3. Do you consider the school you currently work in to be trauma sensitive? Why or why not? If not, what steps could be made to become more trauma sensitive? Think about school rules and consequences, as well as adults in the school that are available to talk to if students need them.
4. Think about your school rules and routines. What are some specific rules or expectations from your class/school that may be confusing or upsetting for new ELLs? How might you address these differences and challenges?

2

How Does Linguistics Impact Teaching and Learning?

Main Points

- ◆ Take time to preview your materials for potential linguistic barriers.
- ◆ ELLs should be exposed to vocabulary multiple times in a variety of contexts.
- ◆ Words often carry multiple meanings; be sure to scan your texts and content in advance.
- ◆ Encourage students to identify cognates.
- ◆ Be cognizant of the amount of figurative language you use during instruction.

Getting Started

Before we begin to examine linguistics in great depth, let's take a step back and think about the English language. *What can make English difficult for someone just learning the language?* One of these difficulties may be the language's rules *(and exceptions to the rules)*. Or, perhaps you thought of words that have different meanings but are spelled or pronounced the same way. In this chapter, we will explore the following *linguistic differences* that may lead to misunderstandings, frustrations or even embarrassing situations:

- ◆ Social vs. academic language
- ◆ Polysemous words

- Prefixes, root words and suffixes
- Homonyms
- Sentence structure
- Prepositions
- Phrasal verbs
- Cognates
- Figurative language/non-literal expressions

Linguistic Difficulties

Social vs. Academic Language

Let's take some time to examine the differences and connections between *social (interpersonal)* and *academic (classroom)* language. We use social language every day to interact with one another: ask for directions, share news, tell stories, make appointments, etc. Students develop a strong command of interpersonal language, often within a year or two of being immersed in English, as there are plenty of opportunities for social interaction both in and outside the school setting. Academic language, on the other hand, is not used in everyday situations, so achieving proficiency is more challenging and takes much longer. Have you ever known an ELL to be quite social on the playground or with his/her peers in the hallway, but be much more quiet and reserved in the classroom setting? Most likely, the reason is that he/she is still acquiring academic language and vocabulary, and may not yet have the proficiency to interact fully in classroom activities and discussions.

While the social layer is mostly oral language and refers to speaking and listening, *academic language* is driven by content and involves all language skills *(listening, speaking, reading and writing)*. It includes scholarly vocabulary, complicated sentence structures and skills like comparing, contrasting, evaluating, synthesizing, inferring and other higher-order thinking skills. Most classroom instruction, assessments, activities and anticipated student-produced projects require a command of both social and academic language. ELLs will need explicit instruction in academic language. Introducing words with visuals and practicing them in a variety of modes and situations can prove to be very effective. We will cover vocabulary instruction in greater depth in Chapter 4.

How do you choose which academic words to teach? A good rule of thumb is to reflect on a recent lesson you taught. Now, summarize it in two sentences and take note of the academic vocabulary you use. *Those are the words you should introduce to the ELLs in your classroom.* Focus on key words for understanding main concepts. This includes vocabulary associated with critical thinking *(describe, compare, etc.)*, assessment *(synthesize, prove, evaluate, etc.)*

and lesson structure *(warm-up, closure, quiz, assessment, etc.)*. The words from the aforementioned categories are *essential* for ELLs to become familiar with in order to gain *access to every day instruction and assessments*.

Exposing students to complicated words in written text, oral directions, teacher presentations, games, word walls, etc. will promote students' vocabulary growth. Encouraging ELLs to use newly-introduced and practiced vocabulary in their speech and writing also proves to be very effective. However, it is important to keep in mind that there is a limit to how many words per lesson is a fair amount to introduce. Depending on students' language proficiency and overall comfort level with a particular academic topic, a range of 5–8 new vocabulary words per lesson is reasonable. So, instead of collecting all the new words from the lesson and expecting students to be successful with that list, identify 5–8 terms that are key words and are crucial to the understanding of a particular lesson and achieving the learning objective(s). It is also important to keep in mind that ELLs require *repeated exposure* to the same list of words throughout the course of several lessons in order for those academic words to become part of their vocabulary. ELLs benefit most from being exposed to the words in a variety of contexts or forms. Using visuals, associations, games, cloze activities, sentence starters and graphic organizers that include the use of the targeted list of words helps ELLs acquire and retain academic vocabulary. Consider introducing vocabulary at the beginning of the week, exposing the students to the words in *various forms* throughout the week as frequently as possible, and then assessing the students' vocabulary knowledge at the end of the week. ELLs' vocabulary tests may look different from native English speakers: the lists may be shorter or visuals may be included. For newcomers who cannot produce sentences yet, labeling images with the correct word from a word bank is an appropriate assessment. For intermediate ELLs, cloze sentences or sentence starters can be used. It is only appropriate for ELLs with advanced or near native-like proficiency to be asked to produce a complex written paragraph using the new vocabulary words.

Polysemous Words

English vocabulary is not always straightforward or easy to learn. Like many other languages in the world, English has words with multiple meanings, called *polysemous* words. Such words present a big challenge for ELLs. Here are a few examples:

Table: furniture *or* a way to organize information.

Foot/feet: body part *or* a unit of measurement.

Formula: baby food *or* something that helps to solve math problems.

Other words that have double or triple meanings are *log, plane, solution, plot* and *character*. Imagine the look on an ELL's face when he/she is asked to write the answer "in the box" and the student is scanning the room for an actual box rather than a designated space on the paper. When introducing new academic vocabulary, take a step back to examine your list for potential confusions. Sometimes, ELLs may have already encountered these words in social settings, but may become confused when they appear in academic content. For instruction, it helps to provide ELLs with photos/illustrations showing the different meanings of the same word.

Such words are best introduced to students using images and contexts. Encourage your ELLs to keep a personal word wall in a folder or a vocabulary journal in a notebook. Vocabulary journals can be divided by subject to help students access the words faster when they need them. The section dividers can be titled: math vocabulary, social studies vocabulary, etc.

Another important point to be made about vocabulary instruction is that it is most helpful to teach new vocabulary along with **word formation patterns.** For example, if you introduce the word *water*, it is important to show students how it can change in a sentence or act as a noun, an adjective, or a verb depending on its function in the sentence:

> *The water is cold. (Noun)*
>
> *The water slide is under construction. (Adjective)*
>
> *I water my plants every day. (Verb)*

After that, ELLs should be introduced to the derivatives of the word *water*: *watering, watered, waters, watery.* Example sentences need to be used to model when each of the forms is used.

> *I am watering my tomato plants now.*
>
> *I watered them yesterday at the same time.*
>
> *His eyes were watery.*
>
> *She waters her garden every morning.*

Prefixes, Root Words and Suffixes

Prefixes, root words and suffixes are small, meaningful parts of words that can help ELLs to recognize more vocabulary. Knowing the meaning of prefixes and suffixes helps students expand their vocabulary and become better at "guessing" the meaning of words based on their parts. Prefixes come before the root word, while suffixes come after the root word. For example, in the word *unhappily,* "*un-*" is the prefix that means "*not*" and "*ly*" is the suffix that turns the word into an adverb, meaning *"possessing the quality of something."* "Happy" is the root word in this case. ELLs benefit from explanations like this because understanding the functions of prefixes and suffixes will help them create and change words by simply adding *"un"* or *"ly."*

Teaching word forms is crucial as students may memorize a word but will only be able to recognize that word in the text when it is used in that one form provided on their vocabulary list. For example, the word *"go"* may be simple to learn, but if a math problem says, *"Michaelene went to the store,"* an ELL may have no idea that *"went"* is a form of *"go"* and has the same meaning but refers to an event in the past. *"Went"* will not be listed in the dictionary under "w" as it is a form of the word "go." An ELL would have no way of finding out those two words are connected without explicit instruction on identifying different forms of the word. Irregular verb charts and irregular plural noun formations are just a few items that need to be explicitly taught to ELLs.

Students can be provided with charts like Tables 2.1 and 2.2 or they can create their own recording words and their forms once they are introduced and practiced. Along with word formation patterns, **prefixes and suffixes** should be introduced when applicable. For example, when teaching the word *realistic*, you can show that <u>un</u>*realistic* means NOT realistic because of the prefix **un-**. After becoming familiar with common prefix meanings, students can apply this knowledge to construct new words using the vocabulary they already have, like *unpredictable, unhappy, unsuccessful, etc.*

Prefix and suffix knowledge also becomes a helpful tool in identifying meanings of unfamiliar words. Some of the most common English prefixes are *un-, re-, in-, dis-, pre-,* and *over-*. Teaching these small but meaningful parts of words

Table 2.1 Example of an Irregular Verb Chart

Present	Past	Participle
buy	bought	bought
go	went	gone
win	won	won

Table 2.2 Example of an Irregular Plural Noun Chart

Singular	Plural
child	children
man	men
tooth	teeth

Table 2.3 Morpheme Chart

Morpheme	Example
Progressive (ing)	Malina is driv**ing**.
Third person singular (s)	Giovanni work**s** at the science center.
Possessive ('s) (s')	Viktoria**'s** favorite animal is lion.
Plural (s, es)	They have box**es** and tool**s**.
Regular past tense (ed)	Steve collect**ed** pens.
Past participle (en)	I have giv**en** Valentina a pencil.

to all students will be beneficial, but ELLs will most benefit from this knowledge and become better equipped to identify word meanings and experiment with building new words. This also proves helpful when students are using a dictionary to find the meaning of a word. *"Unhappy"* may not be in the student's dictionary, but knowing that ***un-*** is a prefix that has a meaning of *"not"* and is just added to the root word *"happy"* will prompt students to look up the word *"happy"* instead and put together the meaning from there. Suffixes are parts of words that are added after the root. Here are some common suffixes:

-*ed* (for past tense) show – showed

-*er* (for comparative adjective) small – smaller

-*er* (for forming a noun from a verb) work – worker

-*est* (for superlative adjectives) small – smallest

-*ly* (for making adverbs out of adjectives) beautiful – beautifully

The morpheme chart (Table 2.3) provides examples of forms to be introduced to ELLs with new vocabulary.

Homonyms

Homonyms are another feature of the English language that proves confusing to both ELLs and native English speakers alike. Homonyms are divided into *homophones* and *homographs*.

Homophones are words that sound the same but may not be spelled the same and have different meanings. ELLs get confused by hearing homophones in oral speech. In addition, homophones are also commonly confused by native speakers in writing, so time spent working on them will be beneficial for all students in your classroom.

Here are a few examples of homophones:

eight – ate

four – for

there – their – they're

to – too – two

<u>Homographs</u> are spelled the same but may or may not be pronounced the same, and, like all homonyms, have different meanings. Here are a few examples of homographs:

wind – wind   *("The <u>wind</u> is strong today." vs. "It is time to <u>wind</u> up your watch.")*

read – read   *(present vs. past tense verb – "I <u>read</u> every day." vs. "I <u>read</u> five books last year.". Additionally, color "red" is a homophone for "read" past tense.*

learned – learned   *("Jimmy learned that information in class." vs. "Jimmy is a learned individual.")*

evening – evening   *(time of day vs. making something smooth)*

One more layer of difficulty with similar sounding words for ELLs is attributed to their inability to hear slight nuances and differences of English sounds. Newcomers first need to learn how to identify and distinguish between different sounds in the English language, especially those that are very close to each other. *What are clearly different sounds to a native speaker's ear may sound the same to ELLs because of their L1 influence.* Some pairs of words may seem confusing to ELLs and words containing such sounds may be mistakenly grouped with homonyms because, to ELLs, these words sound the same:

sit – seat

lick – leak

thick – sick

vote – boat

The inability to hear the difference between these sounds *(referred to as minimal pairs)* impedes listening comprehension as well as speaking proficiency. Unintentionally, students can say something inappropriate, and as a result, can become shy or nervous about practicing speaking in class. It is important to be aware of and sensitive to these difficulties. Modeling proper pronunciation, as opposed to correcting students, is an effective way to target linguistic challenges such as these.

Sentence Structure

Once ELLs acquire some vocabulary, it is time to put the words into phrases and sentences. This is where tense and sentence structure difficulties come in. It is important to point out that English has a lot more tenses than most other languages. When thinking about tenses, one can logically speculate that there should be a past, a present and a future tense, *but did you know that English has 12 tenses in the active voice?*

Let's examine Table 2.4.

How confusing are all these tenses and verb forms for ELLs? In the first year or so, most newcomers will acquire and be able to distinguish between the first two columns: the three simple tenses and the three continuous *(also referred to as progressive)* tenses. The last two columns on the right with the perfect tenses are typically acquired at the intermediate to advanced stages of English language acquisition. It is important to be cognizant of using the simple tenses and sentence structures with ELLs when giving directions, feedback or explaining something new.

Another very important thing to keep in mind is *avoiding passive voice whenever possible*. Passive voice structures are sentences where the subject is not the "doer" of the action, but rather the action is performed by someone or something else and is affecting the subject. See some examples below:

The alliance agreement was signed by the French and the Americans. (Passive voice) – **avoid using this structure with newcomer ELLs.**

The French and the Americans signed the alliance agreement. (Active voice) – **this is a preferred sentence structure to be used with ELLs.**

Table 2.4 English Language Tenses – Active Voice

	Simple	Continuous (Progressive)	Perfect	Perfect Continuous (Progressive)
Present	I **give** lessons	I **am giving** lessons	I **have given** lessons	I **have been** giving lessons
Past	I **gave** lessons	I **was giving** lessons	I **had given** lessons	I **had been giving** lessons
Future	I **will give** lessons	I **will be giving** lessons	I **will have given** lessons	I **will have been** giving lessons

Prepositions

Prepositions tend to cause difficulties for ELLs of all proficiency levels. When students attempt to create phrases and sentences orally or in writing, they often use what they know about prepositions in their L1. English demands the use of a lot of prepositions and sometimes the transfer of the students' L1 knowledge about them is not helpful *(negative transfer)*.

A Russian speaker, for example, will say *"listen music"*, instead of *"listen to music"*, because in Russian, no preposition is necessary after the verb *"listen."* A Spanish speaker is likely to make the mistake of saying *"attend to the meeting"*, rather than *"attend the meeting"*, because the verb "attend" requires a preposition in Spanish. These are just a few examples of ELLs misusing prepositions. Preposition errors don't usually interfere with meaning, *however, meaning is affected when prepositions are misused in phrasal verbs.*

Phrasal Verbs

Phrasal verbs are a prominent feature of the English language. They are verbs with prepositions attached to them to coin a specific meaning. If the preposition is changed, a whole new meaning is acquired. Here are a few examples of phrasal verbs:

> *look = watch or observe something*
>
> *look **after** = take care of*
>
> *look **for** = try to find*
>
> *look **into** = investigate, explore*
>
> *run = move fast*
>
> *run **into** = meet*
>
> *run **after** = chase*
>
> *run **for** (office) = try to get elected*

Phrasal verbs are almost as confusing for ELLs as idiomatic expressions *(figurative language)*. They are also very common in both social and academic language. It's impossible to avoid using phrasal verbs altogether as they are essential in the English language, however, in order to aid ELLs' comprehension, it is important to be cognizant of the difficulties caused by such verbs. When using phrasal verbs in your instruction or explanations, try paraphrasing the sentence using a stand-alone verb (ex: "*__find__ evidence*" instead of "*look for evidence*"). It is also beneficial for students to have a phrasal verb vocabulary wall, folder or dedicated section in their journals.

Other Linguistic Difficulties

Other linguistic difficulties ELLs experience are the *proper use of articles (a/an/the)*, *word order, punctuation, and capitalization.* Articles are not used in every language, so using *a, an* or *the* in front of nouns is a foreign concept to some ELLs. Word order and capitalization rules also differ between many languages.

Special Linguistic Considerations

Cognates

Have you ever seen a word written in a language you do not speak, but you can guess its meaning? Most likely, it was a *cognate*, which is a word that has the same root/origin in two languages. If students are literate in their L1, they are able to more easily recognize cognates, especially in core content areas such as math and science. It is important to note that not all cognates have the same meanings. There are *false cognates* that also exist and can create confusion. For example, in Russian, there is a word *магазин*, pronounced as /*magazine*/. It sounds like the English word *magazine*, but in Russian it actually means "*a store or a shop.*" Another example of a false cognate is the Spanish word "*embarazada,*" which means "*pregnant,*" not "*embarrassed.*" False cognates could easily lead to miscommunication if an ELL unknowingly uses them in speech or writing. There are also *partial cognates,* which are words that have the same meaning in some contexts. Using cognates in class will improve your students' listening and reading comprehension.

Here are a few tips for increasing your students' *cognate awareness*:

- ◆ Scan texts for cognates, locate them and make connections.
- ◆ Create word sorts and dictionary connections.
- ◆ Use read-alouds that contain full cognates.
- ◆ Utilize online resources.
- ◆ Create and update content word walls and sorts with shades of cognates (*full, partial, false*) or have students keep a personalized cognate chart *(see example in Table 2.5).*

Table 2.5 Cognate Chart

Full Cognates	Partial Cognates	False Cognates

Figurative Language/Non-Literal Expressions

Another significant challenge that ELLs face is the use *(and sometimes over-use)* of *figurative language*. A big portion of daily language in English is figurative. One example of figurative language is the use of *idiomatic expressions*. They are cultural and can be impossible to understand for someone who did not grow up within the society that has coined the phrase and uses it frequently. Phrases like *"the grass is greener on the other side"* or *"skating on thin ice"* often cause confusion for ELLs as they try to understand the phrase by translating it word-for-word. Idioms also present problems when students try to express their own thoughts and ideas in speaking or writing. ELLs often include idioms from their native language into their English writing or speaking to make it sound more mature and expressive, but, since they are cultural, they often make no sense when translated into English. An example of this from Russian is *"He is a big pine cone."* What that idiom actually means is "He is an important person." A similar English idiom is *"He is a big fish."* Proficiency in understanding and using idioms comes as one of the last skills in second language acquisition. There is no way for ELLs to tell if something they hear or read is an idiom or a literal expression, so it is vital that you *point them out* and *explain the meaning*. It is also important to be sensitive to students trying to use their L1 idioms in their writing. Instead of dismissing them as nonsensical, have a conversation with the student to figure out what he/she is trying to say. You can then share an English idiom with similar meaning for the student to use instead. This confusion can become a perfect teachable moment.

Tips for Teaching Idioms

- ◆ Ask students to share idioms from their language/culture, while also doing the same in English.
- ◆ Encourage students to record idioms heard in conversations and seen in print.
- ◆ Locate and collect cartoons, comic strips and advertisements that depict the literal version of an idiomatic expression and discuss these with your students.
- ◆ Underline/highlight idioms in newspapers or content area texts and discuss the meanings as they relate to the material/topic.
- ◆ Use published dictionaries of idiomatic sayings and expressions.

By familiarizing yourself with these linguistic differences, you will be better equipped for examining your materials and practice for possible misunderstandings and be able to plan your instruction accordingly.

Reflection Questions

1. Take some time to think about an upcoming unit of study. Identify terms that have multiple meanings. In what ways can you teach these words and their differences in meaning?
2. Brainstorm a creative way to introduce various word forms when teaching vocabulary to ELLs. Think of a specific word *(or a list of words)* and develop several activities that would provide word form exposure.
3. Analyze an excerpt from a text you recently used in class. Look for sentences written in passive voice and change them into active voice.
4. Create a list of phrasal verbs you often use in your instruction. Make a list of synonyms or definitions for those verbs to help ELLs with comprehension.
5. Think of an idiomatic or non-literal expression that you tend to use in class or in your daily language that may cause confusion for ELLs. How would you explain the meaning of this saying to the student?

3

How Can I Bridge the Home/School Connection?

Main Points

- ◆ Organizing events to welcome culturally diverse families into the school helps to familiarize them with the school as well as foster relationships between the families with similar and different backgrounds.
- ◆ Encourage families to continue to speak their native language at home.
- ◆ Evening events and school tours are a great way to make families feel welcome in the school.

Getting Started

As teachers, we know what a vital role parents play in their child's education. Linguistic and cultural barriers exist for ELL families, *but they do not have to stand in the way of building relationships with each other*.

In this chapter, we will explore:

- ◆ Language barriers and tips for working with interpreters.
- ◆ Cultural barriers and differences in schooling around the world.
- ◆ Ideas for building and strengthening relationships with ELL families.
- ◆ Homework challenges and tips.
- ◆ Classroom rewards and recognitions.

Language Barriers

Having a language barrier is one of the greatest inhibitors to ELL families' school involvement. Think about how much paperwork is sent home daily with students: notes about special events, schedule changes, field trip permission slips, family event flyers, club sign-up sheets, newsletters, etc. Imagine trying to sift through this paperwork if it is written in a language you don't understand. Create a *communication folder* that will travel back-and-forth with the student. Separate essential and non-essential communication, and highlight important information, dates and expectations.

Picking up the phone and calling the school when there is a question is rarely an option. Even for parents with intermediate English skills, talking on the phone brings an extra layer of linguistic difficulty, as there are no non-verbal cues they can use to aid their comprehension. Automated phone calls about school closures, delays or early dismissals are often confusing to ELL families with language barriers, and they may come to rely on bilingual friends, community resources or their own children to get that important information whenever possible.

Many school systems have interpreters and translators available, or at least a way of contacting them if a need arises. *Find out if your school or district has access to interpreters/translators and what the process is for requesting one.* Using an interpreter to communicate with parents who speak languages other than English sends a very positive message. It conveys to families that the school cares about their involvement and is reaching out to them in the language they prefer. *It is also important that families know how to request an interpreter on their own.* This will help them to stay connected in the event of an emergency, or simply to stay connected to their child's education.

Interpreters and translators have very different roles. **Interpreters** are called upon when a message needs to be <u>delivered orally</u> *(ex: in-person meetings, phone calls, parent/teacher conferences).* **Translators** are used for the <u>written documents</u> *(ex: behavior and discipline referrals, school flyers, special education paperwork, etc.).* Table 3.1 contains some tips and special considerations to help make your face-to-face meetings a successful and supportive experience, for both you and your ELL families.

Unfortunately, some school systems do not have access to interpreters or translators. They use whatever resources are available to them to reach out to ELL families and relay important information. Online translation websites, community members, foreign language teachers, bilingual staff members, and even students are sometimes used for interpreting and/or translating. *It's important to note that there are many drawbacks to using non-trained people or online programs/apps to deliver messages in languages you do not speak.* Online

Table 3.1 Tips for Working With Interpreters

Tips for Working With Interpreters	Reasons/Benefits
Arrange for an interpreter ahead of time and ask him/her to call and explain to the family that interpretation will be provided during the meeting itself.	Hearing that an interpreter will be attending the meeting may alleviate the family's discomfort about the language barrier and encourage them to attend.
Ask the interpreter to confirm the date, time and location of the meeting with the family a few days before the scheduled date.	Family schedules may be busy and they may need an additional reminder about the meeting. They may also need to ask for time off work or arrange transportation.
Plan for extra time to conduct the meeting.	Every sentence will need to be said twice, once in English and once in the family's native language; the interpreter may need to briefly halt the session to seek clarification on certain terms, cultural differences or any misunderstandings that may occur.
Speak clearly, avoiding professional jargon *(educational terminology)* when possible and address the parents directly, not the interpreter.	Using too many educational terms and/or abbreviations may be confusing and the interpreter will need to stop and seek clarification. Making eye contact with parents and not the interpreter is extremely important. Avoid saying to the interpreter, *"Please tell them I am glad they came today . . ."* and instead address the parents by saying, *"I am glad you came today"* and pause for the interpreter to deliver the message.
Suggest that the interpreter be positioned at a 45 degree angle behind the parent.	This will help you to establish a direct connection with the parent/guardian, and allow the interpreter to focus on facilitating communication instead of being another person in the conversation.
Be mindful of your nonverbal behaviors.	When people do not speak the language, they instinctively look for other clues, like body language and facial expressions to make meaning of the message or try to understand the speaker's attitude towards the message or the subject matter.
Encourage only one person to speak at a time.	This will make the conversation flow better and the interpreter will have an opportunity to relay every message.
Refrain from holding side conversations with other teachers or the interpreter in front of the family.	Be prepared for everything said at the meeting to be interpreted as it is, including side conversations.

Have any important paperwork to be shared during the meeting either translated into the family's native language ahead of time, or ask the interpreter to do a sight translation *(interpreter previews document and paraphrases the key points verbally)*.	It will save time during the meeting if some documents can be translated ahead of time and if the interpreter has time to preview them beforehand and be ready to explain.
Be aware and respectful of cultural differences in discipline, health, family structure and responsibilities.	Keep in mind that differences in school systems exist across the world. This can affect special education practices, cultural perception of school and teachers' roles, school age, school routines, schedules and subjects taught, viewpoints of educational tracks and gender roles.
Provide additional resources/program information as needed.	If you are aware of any community or school resources that may be helpful to the family to know about, be prepared to share.
Don't ask the interpreter for his/her opinion. He/she is there to simply be the voice relaying the message and to foster communication between you and the family.	The interpreter is not an expert on culture, even if he/she comes from the same country/culture, nor is he/she familiar with every family's situation. Address all questions you have to the family directly and encourage the family to ask you *(not the interpreter)* any clarifying questions they have.

translators rarely pick up on the context of a message. Consequently, for words with multiple meanings, the program/app chooses a word randomly as opposed to the one that belongs in the actual context of the sentence. To test out how awkward or skewed a message can come out when using online translation sites, input a message in English and ask for it to be translated into another language. Then, copy the text that came out in that language and have it translated back into English. You will see how the message often gets lost or confused by just a few key words that did not translate the way they were intended.

Another popular source for interpretation and translation is a foreign language teacher or a bilingual staff member or parent in the building. Remember, being bilingual does not make someone an automatic interpreter. Even when someone speaks another language, he/she may lack the appropriate training or enough language proficiency to deliver a school specific message, especially if it involves educational terms, safety concerns or urgent behavioral/disciplinary matters. Also, be sure to avoid asking students to interpret for their own parents or parents of a classmate. This skews family roles and severely compromises the message to be delivered. There is no guarantee that what you are saying is going to be interpreted accurately and remain confidential if a student is used. *The best way to communicate with families when there is a language barrier is always through a trained interpreter whenever possible.*

Cultural Barriers and Differences in Schooling Around the World

One of the first steps towards building a strong home/school connection is to be sensitive to any potential cultural differences that may exist. In some countries, educational decisions are left to the schools, and the parents' job is to care for their children at home. Other reasons that prevent some families from actively participating in the education process might include language barriers, work schedules or lack of understanding of how schooling works in the United States.

Education systems around the world operate differently. Things like grading, daily schedules, school rules, behavior expectations, curriculum, lunch and parent involvement can be confusing for ELL families. Below is a list of **differences in schooling around the world**. These examples are not specific to any particular country, but rather a collection of differences to be aware of. It is important to note that *assumptions cannot be made.* Families from the same country may have very different cultural and schooling experiences. Communication with your families and the ELL specialist is key in learning which differences exist.

- ◆ School age *(in some countries students start school much older or younger than in the US; the same goes for average graduation age).*
- ◆ Compulsory attendance requirement.
- ◆ Grading system *(point value system, private nature of grading)*; credits towards graduation *(how many are required for a diploma and that simply attending school does not guarantee graduation/diploma)*; GPA *(how it's calculated and why it's important)*; and state testing requirements.
- ◆ Leveling of classes and course selection process.
- ◆ Inclusion of all students *(families may come from countries where students with learning or physical disabilities are not mainstreamed).*
- ◆ School staff *(many families are unfamiliar with the jobs of school counselors, psychologists, behavior specialists, special education teachers, gifted education teachers, ELL staff etc.).*
- ◆ Typical school day *(schedule, special areas, remaining at school through the lunch period).*
- ◆ School bus transportation *(routes, bus behavior, the fact that it's free, etc.).*
- ◆ Classroom set up *(small/whole group instruction, seating arrangement, instructional materials used).*

- Appropriate school clothing.
- Level of parental involvement in school decisions (*parent/teacher conferences, meetings, etc.*).

Building and Strengthening Relationships With ELL Families

Think proactively. Now that you know what the barriers are and can anticipate for them, it's time to plan ways to better connect with your ELL families.

Make a time to meet with your ELL specialist and your school administrators to brainstorm ideas for increasing ELL family involvement. Here are a few ideas to get you started:

- *Arrange a school tour* with your ELL families that explains how things are set up, what their child's day at school looks like, differences in schooling and how learning can be supported at home. This will also allow an opportunity for parents to ask questions they may have about the school.
- *Familiarize parents with classroom routines.* Invite them to shadow you for a day, or create a photobook or video that shows snapshots from a typical day.

Table 3.2 Parent Survey

Parent Survey *(We invite all parents to participate in this survey).*
Child's name: Parent/guardian(s) name(s):
1. What expectations and hopes do you have for your child for this school year and beyond?
2. What are your child's interests and hobbies?

(continued)

Table 3.2 continued

3. What is one thing you would like the school to know about your child?
4. Would you be available and interested to visit your child's class? If yes, how would you prefer to help (check all that apply): ☐ Read to the class ☐ Help with hands-on projects ☐ Chaperone a field trip ☐ Watch my child learning ☐ Other_____
5. How can the school support you?
6. What questions do you have for your teachers or school administrators?
7. It is best to contact me by: ☐ Phone ☐ Email ☐ Note in my child's backpack ☐ Text message
8. Here is my contact information:
9. My preferred language of communication is:

◆ *Rethink traditional back-to-school nights and other school-wide events.* Schedule an interpreter to reach out to ELL families ahead of time. Invite them in for a small meet-and-greet group session prior to the main event. Explore options for providing dinner, as this may encourage more families to attend. If your school has a high ELL population, consider holding an *ELL Family Night*, where you can explore different topics and connect them to community resources.

◆ ***Gather information from your ELL families.*** Consider having parents complete a survey at your next evening event. This way, an interpreter can assist *(see Table 3.2)*.

Homework Challenges and Suggestions

As teachers, we hope *(and often assume)* that parents/guardians are willing and able to help with homework or school projects. This is often difficult when a language barrier is present. Family members may be familiar with the concepts but unable to read or understand the English directions. Simple tasks like practicing rhyming or initial letter identification with young learners can become impossible for parents with little knowledge of the English language. Let's give it a try ourselves. Take a look at the example of such a task in Table 3.3.

Unless you speak Russian this task was probably impossible for you. The assignment, however, was simple: *"Circle the words that start with the same letter as the word in the picture."* The problem here was not just accessing the directions but also knowing what the words are and how they are spelled in that language. So, in the first row of words, the word for sun is с̲олнце, so страна (country) is the correct answer as they both begin with "с." In the second row, cat is к̲от in Russian, therefore the correct answer is к̲рыша as both begin with a "к."

Imagine how adults might feel when their child is asking them for help with a homework assignment they can't understand. The feeling of helplessness and intimidation can overwhelm a parent who is unable to help with such "simple" homework. To make homework more accessible to ELLs linguistically, use direct language (avoiding idioms), simple phrases, short and clear directions. To ensure the task is understood, it helps when teachers model the outcome of the assignments, or at least start each assignment together with the students in class. This way, when the child gets home and starts working on homework, he/she knows what to do independently. *Remember, the purpose of homework should be review and reinforcement, not new learning.* One of the best things you can do is to have a brief conversation with your ELL after each homework assignment. Find out how much time it took him/her to complete it, and if there is anyone at home that helped out. This information will guide you in assigning an appropriate amount/complexity level of homework. When assigning homework to ELLs, teachers need to keep in mind that parental assistance is not always possible. Parents may simply not have the time or linguistic ability to help with homework. In addition, some older ELLs may have important family responsibilities

Table 3.3

Обведите слова, которые начинаются с такой же буквы как и слово, изображенное на картинке:			
	девочка	мальчик	страна
	стакан	крыша	город

like babysitting younger siblings, caring for the elderly or working an evening job. These factors need to be considered when assigning and grading homework. Getting to know your students and their families is of high importance.

Valuing every family's native language is a very important message teachers need to send to the parents. Often, families feel that the use of their L1 at home inhibits their child's progress in learning English. *This is not so*. Parents need to hear from educators that providing their child with rich language experiences at home, no matter which language is used, benefits their child's development. Reading books to their children, asking questions and having discussions about movies, books, the news, etc. in their native language will promote students' intellectual and linguistic development. Skills children acquire in their L1 will eventually transfer to their L2 when their English proficiency catches up.

Classroom Rewards and School Recognitions

Recognizing ELLs' growth and accomplishments is important. We want students to feel successful and valued. Oftentimes, teachers give tangible prizes like pencils, eraser toppers, stickers or other small and inexpensive items, or praise students by announcing their name and accomplishment for the whole class to hear. It is important to note that reinforcements and rewards such as these are not always universally perceived as positive. Some ELLs and their families may feel intimidated or confused to be given a prize for their school work or hear their name announced in front of the class. However, this does not mean that recognizing student accomplishment is not a good idea for ELLs and their families – just be sure to take the extra step to *make sure both families and students understand what awards and recognitions are for and how students can earn them*. Positive phone calls home with the help of interpreters can also be used to communicate student successes in the classroom and promote a conversation about school at home.

Reflection Questions

1. Imagine if your child had higher language proficiency skills than you and he/she was in charge of certain tasks *(think about shopping, answering the phone, learning the news, being involved in school, understanding and paying the bills, etc.)*. How different would your life be?
2. Fill in Table 3.4. Interview some of your colleagues to find more information about the ways they make connections with culturally and linguistically diverse parents.

Table 3.4

How do I currently involve ELL families? *(Or plan to involve)*
What are some creative "outside the box" ideas I have for increasing ELL family involvement?

3. Imagine that you have an ELL family that has been unable to come into school. How might you provide them with a "glimpse" into their child's school day?
4. Have you been in a meeting where an interpreter was used? Reflect on information shared in this chapter and what you might be able to do differently next time.
5. Imagine that you have been tasked with planning an ELL Family Night. What information would you share? How would the event look?

Part II

Where to Go – Instruction and Beyond

4

What Should My Instruction and Assessment Look Like?

Main Points

- ◆ There are key steps to consider when planning instruction and assessment.
- ◆ Pairing content and language objectives is critical.
- ◆ Use vocabulary activities and games to deepen students' understanding of academic language.
- ◆ Assessment methods should always match instructional practices.
- ◆ Grades should not be a reflection of language level.

Getting Started

Let's begin this chapter with a few words of advice. Having an ELL in your class *does not mean that you have to reinvent the wheel*. ELLs can participate in meaningful instruction before they can demonstrate native or near-native language proficiency. With that said, there is no need to create a whole different lesson plan. In this chapter, we will explore how to make your content accessible for ELLs and examine best practices for instructing and assessing your ELLs.

There are five key steps to consider when planning your instruction and assessment:

Step 1: Get to know your ELLs.

Step 2: Choose the essentials to be taught and plan accordingly.

Step 3: Modify your content to ensure accessibility.

Step 4: Explore new methods for teaching vocabulary.

Step 5: Examine your assessment methods.

Step 1: Get to Know Your ELLs

The first step in the process is to examine specifics about your students. Start with a conversation with your ELL specialist. Refer to Chapter 6 *(Table 6.2)* and Chapter 7 *(Table 7.1)* for some helpful data and background information collection tools. Remember, one of the most important pieces of information that will guide your lesson planning is your students' *English language proficiency levels*. Find out when the last language assessment was, and what levels students are in reading, writing, listening and speaking. Once you know these levels, take some time to examine what is reasonable to expect from your learner at each of these levels in relation to your content. Utilize district- and state-specific documents that outline this information. This will help to guide the language objectives that you will pair with your content objectives.

Step 2: Choose the Essentials to Be Taught and Plan Accordingly

You may be asking yourself, *"Where do I begin?"* This is a common question all classroom teachers have when thinking about lesson planning for ELLs. The most important thing to remember is that what is good teaching for all learners in your classroom is *essential teaching* for ELLs. So, what is considered good teaching? It starts with planning for individual student needs and levels, representing content in different ways, providing students with multiple paths and opportunities to demonstrate their knowledge and adapting your instruction and assessments as needed. The same instructional practices that work best for your non-ELLs are equally effective for your ELLs.

Take Time for Two!
Take a step back and look at your students and your upcoming units of study. Ask yourself these two simple, yet essential and interconnected questions:

1. **What are the most essential pieces my students need in order to prepare them for the next level of content?**
   This can be a daunting task at first, as all content within your curriculum is important. The best place to start is by examining each unit of study before you teach it. Identify the key vocabulary terms and concepts that students will need to know in order to be

engaged in meaningful instruction. Even in the beginning stages of learning English, students are able to demonstrate what they are learning if given appropriate opportunities, with the help of teachers removing linguistic barriers from both instruction and assessments. Good teachers begin with the end in mind and plan instruction and assessment accordingly.

2. **How will my student(s) language levels and culture affect my teaching?**

The instructional changes you will be making for your newcomers with no English skills will look very different from the changes needed for an intermediate or advanced level ELL. Keeping in constant communication with your ELL specialist is important for exchanging information about students' current English proficiency levels and the depth of their content knowledge. You may discover that an ELL has extensive background knowledge and interest in your content area, or, on the contrary, has extensive academic gaps that need to be addressed before the information you present in class makes any sense to him/her. Being the content expert of your subject area, you can take a few steps back and address these gaps one-on-one or in a small group setting. It is important to keep in mind that the ELL specialist is teaching the language through your content, so sharing materials both ways is the most productive approach.

Step 3: Modify Your Content to Ensure Accessibility

ELLs should not be removed from the challenges set forth by the standards but supported in meeting them. *So what exactly does that look like?* The first word that should come to mind is *"access."* ELLs should have access to grade-level curriculum and receive the necessary support to help them engage in the content. Instruction should build on students' existing funds of knowledge *(L1, background knowledge, interests and motivations)* in order to expand them. Modifications and accommodations should be put in place to help increase accessibility.

Modifications vs. Accommodations

The term *modification i*s often used interchangeably with *accommodation*, but the two are quite different. *Modifications are changes in the construct of the material*. This includes altered language load and reduction in both content and cognitive complexity. Modifications are changes a teacher can make to his/her instruction that supports students in comprehending and retaining material, as well as demonstrating their knowledge. Adding images and photos to a presentation is an example of a modification. Another example of modification can be adding a word box or images to a vocabulary quiz. Specialists at your school (ELL, special education, ELA, math) are a great resource for modification ideas and suggestions. Check in with them often, as they may have already modified certain assignments and assessments. *Modifications are necessary for ELL success.* All assignments, including assessments, can be modified by including images, charts, graphs, graphic organizers, eliminating answer choices, simplifying the linguistic complexity of questions and answer choices and providing word banks, sentence starters, etc.

The following are some basic *modification* strategies:

◆ Providing scaffolding, graphic organizers, timelines, charts, bilingual dictionaries, word banks.
◆ Teaching organizational skills.
◆ Providing highlighted texts, chapter summaries and copies of notes that outline main points.
◆ Breaking assignments into manageable chunks and providing extra time to complete projects/assessments.
◆ Providing digital support options.
◆ Limiting answer choices and distractors.
◆ Offering nonverbal opportunities for students to demonstrate understanding (matching, sequencing, fill-in-the-blank).
◆ Giving open-book and open-note tests.
◆ Asking students to restate concepts (orally or in writing) and read content aloud.
◆ Requiring shorter written responses to items (respond in a sentence or two rather than paragraphs).
◆ Simplifying directions in English as much as possible (avoiding the use of idiomatic expressions or passive voice sentences) and pointing out words that have multiple meanings in different contexts.
◆ Avoiding texts using local dialects, which can cause confusion *(also be cognizant of your own regional dialect)*.
◆ Allowing opportunities for collaboration with native English speaking peers.
◆ Recapping important ideas at the end of your lesson.

Accommodations change the way a student accesses instruction or assessment. Accommodation documents are state-specific legal documents that are mutually agreed upon and signed by teachers, administrators and parents. This documentation lists specific *(and often limited)* changes that must be provided to identified students during instruction and assessment. Some of the most common ELL accommodations include extended time, use of bilingual synonym dictionary, verbatim reader and scribe.

Collaborate with your ELL specialist to choose appropriate modifications and accommodations based on students' proficiency levels, academic histories and grade level. Keep in mind that language development is always happening. Be sure to revisit agreed upon modifications and accommodations throughout the year and make changes as your ELLs advance in their English language development.

Step 4: Explore New Methods for Teaching Vocabulary

You are probably familiar with the term "frontloading." Often times, classroom teachers will focus on a limited amount of key words and pre-teach these words to ELLs before they encounter content. Unfortunately, *"frontloading" often involves teaching vocabulary without context or connections* and, therefore, it isn't always the most effective method. As educators, the challenge is to move away from traditional vocabulary instruction and activities that focus on pre-teaching content and preparing students to "survive" in class, to providing rich, multifaceted activities and experiences that encourage students to make real-life connections and gain a deeper understanding of the content. Instead of thinking, "what vocabulary words does this student need to know in order to be successful," ask yourself, *"what language experiences does this student need to successfully master the content?"*

Take a minute to think about how you learned new vocabulary in a second language. What stuck? What didn't? Why is this? If you have traveled to a country where that language was spoken, you may have quickly realized that a few years of foreign language instruction didn't prepare you for an in-depth content discussion with a native speaker. Students need *explicit vocabulary instruction delivered in a meaningful manner*. Learning vocabulary in isolation just doesn't work. Let's face it, most students don't go home and discuss the academic language they are learning *(although as teachers, we would love to see this happen)*. It is our job as educators to provide them with rich, interconnected, real world language experiences.

When teaching vocabulary to ELLs, there are *five essential tips* to consider:

1. **Repeated exposure is key.** ELLs need to encounter words multiple times in a variety of contexts in order to fully learn them. Provide repeated exposures as often as possible. Be explicit about the words you are pre-selecting, and continue to expose your ELLs to key vocabulary before, during and after reading.

2. **Activate prior knowledge and make content/experience connections.** Students learn best when they can make connections to real-world applications. Include interdisciplinary connections that actively engage your learners. Working together with other content teachers and the ELL specialist is key, as discussed in Chapter 6. Showing students how to make connections and associations to help remember word meanings is also very helpful. Students then will make their own associations or connections to their experiences in order to cement the new vocabulary words into their memory.

3. **Utilize high-quality visuals and instructional materials.** Visuals are critical to helping ELLs learn new words. Photographs and high-quality visuals should be used in all content lessons. This will enable students to make meaningful connections with the content as well as their prior experiences. After that, students can be encouraged to create their own visuals connected to each vocabulary word.

4. **Provide meaningful language experiences and draw attention to irregular words.** Language learning is a continuum. It is essential to provide language experiences and activities that focus on an integration of content and key vocabulary. When students answer questions during the lesson or engage in discussions, encourage them to use the key vocabulary written on the board. Another helpful thing to do is have students point to the word(s) on a list, locate them on a vocabulary wall and state what each word means. Be sure to draw students' attention to irregular words. Let's use the basic word *"go"* to demonstrate this. If you say the following past tense sentence, *"He went to the library"*, the word *"go"* changes into an unrecognizable *"went"*. Most common transformations that are difficult to recognize happen to irregular verbs and nouns with irregular plural formation *(see examples below)*:

> <u>Irregular verbs:</u>
> bring – brought
> teach – taught
> sing – sang
> give – gave
>
> <u>Nouns with irregular plural formations:</u>
> ox – oxen
> child – children
> man – men
> person – people
> mouse – mice
> louse – lice

Table 4.1 Knowledge Rating Scale

Word	I know what it means and can give several examples	I recognize the word, and I know it has something to do with . . .	I have heard this word before, but I don't know what it means	I have never seen or heard this word before

As you see, words like these can be very confusing to students who are learning them for the first time. If your ELLs use a bilingual dictionary to locate unfamiliar words, irregulars are not easily locatable, which creates another layer of challenge. This is why it is essential to plan activities where students will encounter irregular words in different forms and various contexts.

5. **Assess what students know and encourage them to do the same.** It is important to realize that assessing vocabulary knowledge is more complicated than just gauging whether or not students know certain words. It involves being able to assess if students can apply them correctly in both social and academic settings. Consider the use of a knowledge rating scale *(see Table 4.1)* that students can use as a pre or post self-assessment tool. Students who check that they already know and can use a particular word during pre-assessment can become the teacher's "resident experts" and can be called upon to explain and provide examples or images illustrating the words.

Easy to Create Vocabulary Activities and Games!

Remember, an ELL needs to encounter a word multiple times in a variety of contexts in order to learn and apply it. The following are content vocabulary games and activities that are easy and quick to plan, create and implement in any classroom. Keep in mind that these activities can be used with all learners, not just ELLs. The materials you will need are basic, inexpensive and most likely you already have them in your classroom!

Table 4.2 Brain Dump!

Description: This is similar to brainstorming but the difference is that students use words only, not phrases or sentences. This activity can be used as a pre-assessment before starting a new topic, or to help students gather ideas for writing.
Materials needed: • Pencils, pens or markers • Large chart paper • Content resources
How to play: 1. Provide students with a topic and a blank piece of chart paper. 2. In small groups, ask students to write down words and pictures related to the topic. 3. Ask guided questions to encourage discussion. 4. Post the papers around the room and encourage students to visit each and discuss. 5. Use as a springboard for writing.
How might you use, adapt or extend this in your classroom?
How will you group students for this activity?
What questions can you plan that will encourage critical thinking?

Table 4.3 Café Talk!

Description: This is a versatile activity and can be used for any content area. Students can either identify words or phrases related to content-relevant photos or write extended sentences. They may also choose to elaborate more on a picture they feel more knowledgeable about, or one they feel is a more powerful image. It is helpful if the vocabulary is recorded on the board as a "menu" for students to choose from when describing the photos. If used towards the end of the unit, students can be tasked with incorporating as many of the key vocabulary words into their writing.
Materials needed: • Pencils, pens or markers • Photos that reflect content • Chart paper or large sticky notes • Glue (if using chart paper)

How to play:

1. Glue four different photos on a piece of chart paper (see below) and place in the middle of a table. If you have a large class, you can duplicate the chart paper or choose four new photos for each table. *If space is an issue, use large sticky notes attached to the bottom of each photo and pass them around the room.*
2. Place students into pairs or groups of three, starting each group at a different photo.
3. Students will look at the photos, discuss them with one another and write ideas, phrases and/ or sentences about each. Students will then rotate around the table to look at the next photo, adding more information to the other groups' writing.
4. Debrief as a whole group. Have students choose the most powerful photo and synthesize the information.
5. Extend the content as desired.

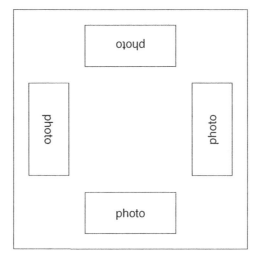

How might you use, adapt or extend this in your classroom?

How will you group students for this activity?

What questions can you plan that will encourage critical thinking?

Table 4.4 Content Webs!

Description: We have all used webs as graphic organizers. It starts with the main idea or a topic in the middle and with related words added all around. Webs can be challenging as they are full of unfamiliar terms and are often devoid of visuals. This activity pairs words, pictures and descriptions! It also encourages academic conversations using target vocabulary.
Materials needed: • Pencils, pens or markers • Sticky notes • Index cards • Paper bags • Pictures/photos • Paper
How to play: 1. Prepare bags that contain pictures/photos/words related to the topic. Include one blank index card and lots of blank sticky notes. 2. Place students in small groups. They pull all the items out of their bags, arrange the photos and words around the blank index card. They then collaborate to identify the topic/theme and write it down on the index card. 3. Students then use different sized sticky notes to attach to the pictures, photos and words to provide additional information, labels and explanations. The webs can then be glued to a large piece of chart paper and displayed in the room or used as a springboard for writing.
How might you use, adapt or extend this in your classroom?
How will you group students for this activity?
What questions can you plan that will encourage critical thinking?

Table 4.5 Crack the Clues!

Description: This is a great way to pair content and language objectives together while encouraging students to think critically, work collaboratively and deepen their understanding of content.
Materials needed: • Pencils, pens or markers • Index cards

How to play:

1. Create index cards that have 4–5 clues about one term (ex: the first letter is_____, the last letter is_____, the definition is_____, a photo/picture, number of syllables is_____). All the clues lead only to one term.
2. Students are placed in small groups. Each group is given several sets of clue cards.
3. Students within each group take it in turns to read the cards aloud, work as a team to crack the clues and determine what the terms are.

The 1st letter is _____	The word has _____ syllables
The last letter is _____	The definition is _____

How might you use, adapt or extend this in your classroom?

How will you group students for this activity?

What questions can you plan that will encourage critical thinking?

Table 4.6 Envelope Exchange!

Description: This vocabulary review activity starts as an independent or paired task that can be turned into a center activity, partner work or a concept review packet. These can then be used to support writing or as a center activity.

Materials needed:

- Pencils, pens or markers
- Sticky notes

(continued)

Table 4.6 continued

• Text selections and content resources • Envelopes • Scissors • Paper

How to play:

1. Have students divide a piece of paper into nine sections and provide students with a topic.
2. Give students three categories to write on sticky notes and attach them to the top of the sheet of paper *(see the image below)*. The categories can vary based on age, level and content area *(category examples include word, picture, definition, examples, non-examples)*.
3. Students use their resources *(notes, dictionaries, glossaries, footnotes in the readings, etc.)* to explore key vocabulary around the topic and complete their sheet.
4. Students then cut up their grid, place the pieces of paper in an envelope and exchange them with another student who can then try to match them up. The envelopes can be used to support writing or as a center activity.

Word	Meaning	Picture

How might you use, adapt or extend this in your classroom?

How will you group students for this activity?

What questions can you plan that will encourage critical thinking?

Table 4.7 Find Someone Who!

Description: This activity provides opportunities for content review as well as peer teaching. This activity is equally great for a pre-assessment or at the end of a lesson or unit. Elevate this activity by tasking students to both develop and solve the problems. Newcomer ELLs can easily participate by making picture problems or working with a partner when possible.

Materials needed:

- Pencils, pens or markers
- Paper

How to play:

Method #1 – <u>Teacher creates the handout:</u>

1. Create a handout with nine sections (each one containing a different problem or content task).
2. Students rotate around the room, discuss the content and solve the problems with one another.
3. Students listen to their peers and record their responses. Have students "sign off" on the section when they have solved a problem.

Method #2 – <u>Students create the handout:</u>

1. Students divide a piece of paper into nine sections.
2. In each section, students create problems or fill in the blank questions around the chosen content area.
3. Students rotate around the room, discuss the content and solve problems with one another.
4. Students listen to their peers and record their responses. Have students "sign off" on the section when they have solved a problem.

Find Someone Who . . .

Recalls yesterday's key math vocabulary	Can solve $17 + 26$	Can draw an example of $22 - 19$

How might you use, adapt or extend this in your classroom?

How will you group students for this activity?

What questions can you plan that will encourage critical thinking?

Table 4.8 Gallery Walk and Talk!

Description: This activity is great for reviewing concepts when there are multiple ways to approach and solve a problem. The important part of this activity is not so much the initial task of solving the problem as a group, but rather the "talk" portion where other groups' problems and solutions are explored. This activity also elicits a great deal of oral discussions using content vocabulary.
Materials needed: • Different colored markers (one color per group) • Large chart paper
How to play: 1. Divide the students into groups and assign each group a different problem written on chart paper to discuss and solve. 2. Students then rotate around the room and "gallery walk", reading other groups' problems and responses. Each group has a specific colored marker and writes feedback, different ways to solve the problem, etc. on each chart as they rotate around the room.
How might you use, adapt or extend this in your classroom?
How will you group students for this activity?
What questions can you plan that will encourage critical thinking?

Table 4.9 Give One, Get One!

Description: This activity is great for helping with brainstorming, as students have the opportunity to exchange ideas with one another. As students rotate, their lists grow. This activity is great for previewing the next unit of study and also activating the students' prior knowledge.
Materials needed: • Pencils, pens or markers • Sticky notes or index cards
How to play: 1. Give each student a sticky note or index card and have them write the numbers one to ten (or more) in list format. 2. Have each student write one to two examples on their own card around a given topic. 3. Students then move around the room exchanging ideas and examples. It's okay for ideas to be passed "through" to other students when they are stuck. 4. After an appropriate amount of time, have students compare their lists, prioritize and categorize ideas etc.

How might you use, adapt or extend this in your classroom?
How will you group students for this activity?
What questions can you plan that will encourage critical thinking?

Table 4.10 Guess That Word!

Description: This activity gets students using new vocabulary words in sentences, and exposes them to different forms of words (plurals, tenses, etc.). This activity works great for more abstract and academic words, but can also be used with younger learners for concrete words.
Materials needed: • Pencils, pens or markers   • Pre-written index cards (with one key vocabulary term per card)
How to play: 1. Assign each student (or group of students) several index cards with terms written on them. On the blank side of the card, have them draw a picture that represents the meaning of the term.   2. Collect the cards and randomly choose a few to project through a document camera. Students discuss the pictures and guess the terms. Model the use of the words in sentences and explain what part of speech each is and how it may change.   3. Encourage students who guess incorrectly to make an argument for why he/she thought it was a different term.   4. Repeat the activity throughout the unit of study.
How might you use, adapt or extend this in your classroom?
How will you group students for this activity?
What questions can you plan that will encourage critical thinking?

Table 4.11 I Have, Who Has?

Description: This activity is great for exploring many key terms around a given topic. It also provides students with oral discourse opportunities.
Materials needed: • Pencils, pens or markers • Index cards • Content-based resources
How to play: Method #1 – <u>Teacher creates the cards:</u> 1. Create cards with content words and/or pictures with an answer on the top and a question on the bottom and distribute them to students. See examples of the cards below. Connect all the cards to one another so the question on one card is solved by the answer on another. 2. Select any student to begin by reading his/her entire card. "I have ___. Who has ___?" 3. The student with the solution to the question reads his/her card, "I have ____. Who has ____?" 4. Continue until all students have read their cards. <table><tr><td>I have an acute angle.</td><td>I have an obtuse angle.</td><td>I have a right angle.</td></tr><tr><td>Who has an angle that is more than 90 degrees?</td><td>Who has an angle that is exactly 90 degrees?</td><td>Who has . . . ?</td></tr></table> Method #2 – <u>Students create the cards:</u> 1. Give each student two index cards. Direct students to choose one term and write the definition on one index card, while drawing a picture of it on the second card. 2. Collect all the cards, shuffle and redistribute to the class. 3. Select any student to begin by reading his/her entire card aloud or describing the picture. The student who has the match then says "I have it!" They then share their second card and around the room it goes.
How might you use, adapt or extend this in your classroom?
How will you group students for this activity?
What questions can you plan that will encourage critical thinking?

Table 4.12 Important Words!

Description: This is a great "get acquainted" activity that you can use with students and even parents. It will help you learn about values, beliefs and prior experiences.
Materials needed: • Pencils, pens or markers • Sticky notes
How to play: 1. Have students think of a word that is important to them. Provide an example that you have created. Ask them to write it down and/or draw a picture of it on a sticky note. 2. They then share their words with one another and discuss why they are important to them. 3. Use as a writing extension.
How might you use, adapt or extend this in your classroom?
How will you group students for this activity?
What questions can you plan that will encourage critical thinking?

Table 4.13 Key Word Capture!

Description: This is a great activity to do during reading and works well with content-based fiction and non-fiction texts. While students read, they focus on comprehension as they are tasked with choosing words that are important. It is also a valuable activity since students get to discuss their choices and argue their perspectives of why certain words may or may not belong in a group together.
Materials needed: • Pencils, pens or markers • Sticky notes • Text selections • Paper
How to play: 1. Place students in pairs or groups of three. Provide a reading selection and 5–10 sticky notes to each group. 2. As students read, they select 5–10 content words that they feel are important to the understanding of the selection. They record these words on separate sticky notes. 3. Students discuss their words, sort them into categories and create a group or class bar graph showing the number of times words have been chosen by the students, and the different categories of the words they have selected.

(continued)

Table 4.13 continued

4. Discuss the findings and reasons why the students selected those particular words. 5. Students generate a summary statement/main idea of the selection. 6. Use as a springboard for writing.
How might you use, adapt or extend this in your classroom?
How will you group students for this activity?
What questions can you plan that will encourage critical thinking?

Table 4.14 A Mile a Minute!

Description: This activity should be done with content photos/pictures around a given topic. The answers you are trying to elicit can be either very specific or open to personal interpretation. This activity is also great for vocabulary review.
Materials needed: • A master set of photos (content terms) • Document camera
How to play: 1. Divide students into pairs and arrange them so Partner A can see the screen, but Partner B cannot. 2. Display content images. Partner A must describe each picture for Partner B without saying what it is. Partner B should eventually guess what Partner A is describing. 3. Rotate around the room, which will give you insight into students' knowledge of the topic.
How might you use, adapt or extend this in your classroom?
How will you group students for this activity?
What questions can you plan that will encourage critical thinking?

Table 4.15 Music Mixing!

Description: Get your students moving with music and discussion! This is a great activity in listening and speaking!
Materials needed: • Music
How to play: 1. Play music and get students moving around the room. 2. Stop the music and call out a number (ex: 2, 3, 4). Students need to quickly form groups of that number of people. If there are extra students left, encourage them to join whichever group they would like to. 3. Call out a discussion topic and give them time to talk. 4. Start the music again and repeat the process.
How might you use, adapt or extend this in your classroom?
How will you group students for this activity?
What questions can you plan that will encourage critical thinking?

Table 4.16 "Picture Walk Prediction"

Description: This activity is an adaptation to the traditional picture walk. It is best to choose a text that is heavy with visuals/photos. This activity will also help you to identify students' interests within the parameters of a given topic, as well as give insight into prior knowledge and experiences related to the subject matter.
Materials needed: • Pencils, pens or markers • Sticky notes • Text for picture walk • Document camera • Paper
How to play: 1. Picture walk (display the images for the students to see) from a text but do not read the words. Ask students to call out words they predict the author will use in the text.

(continued)

Table 4.16 continued

2. After finishing the picture walk, have the class share 5–10 words aloud that they heard a neighbor say *(record these on a sheet of paper or the board)*.
3. Break students into small groups or pairs and ask them to brainstorm 10–15 additional words that they predict the author will use in the text. They may not use the 5–10 words that you already recorded. Each group will record their words on separate sticky notes.
4. Each group is then given three strips of different colored paper. They will then examine their group's list of words and record the following on each strip of paper:
 	
   • 1 word they predict all groups have in common
   • 1 word they feel is special and unique to their group
   • 1 word that they want to learn more about
 	
5. Each group chooses a representative. The representatives form a line or circle around the room and take turns to share their words from one of the above categories. The procedure is repeated for each of the three categories.
6. Discuss connections across groups (same words, unique words, etc.).

How might you use, adapt or extend this in your classroom?
How will you group students for this activity?
What questions can you plan that will encourage critical thinking?

Table 4.17 Visual Vocabulary!

Description: This is a great way to make word walls come alive! Student-created pictures serve as a visual representation of meaning. If images are paired with letters that are out of order or staggered randomly *(see examples below)*, be sure that students write the word out correctly somewhere on the card. 

symmetry ┊ ʎɹʇǝmmʎƨ

Materials needed:

- Pencils, pens or markers
- Sticky notes or index cards

How to play:

1. Students draw a content word in a way that represents the meaning, including the actual word itself within their drawing.
2. Post them on content word walls or place at learning stations throughout the classroom.

How might you use, adapt or extend this in your classroom?

How will you group students for this activity?

What questions can you plan that will encourage critical thinking?

Table 4.18 What's the Word?

Description: This activity can easily be turned into a game with points awarded and several groups competing, or it can simply be used as a vocabulary and concept review before a unit assessment.
Materials needed: • Dry erase boards and markers
How to play: 1. Place students in small groups. 2. Each group chooses one person to send out the room. Once the chosen student leaves, their group must decide on one content word, which they then write or draw on their dry erase board. 3. When the student returns to the room, the dry erase board is displayed behind the student so the class can see, but the student cannot. 4. The student's job is to guess the word by asking either "yes/no," or open-ended questions.

(continued)

Table 4.18 continued

How might you use, adapt or extend this in your classroom?
How will you group students for this activity?
What questions can you plan that will encourage critical thinking?

Table 4.19 Word Windows!

Description: These cards can replace the traditional vocabulary study lists. Instead of being given an already prepared list of words, students spend time creating these, which provides them with more authentic exposure to key vocabulary. It also requires them to think critically about words and their uses. This is a great adaptation to the traditional word cards/word rings, which typically only use one side of the card. Since these are double-sided, students can quiz themselves at home while reviewing vocabulary.
Materials needed: • Pencils, pens or markers • Index cards
How to play: 1. Students write a content term on the front of an index card. 2. They then divide the other side of the index card into four sections and record each of the following within the sections: formal definition, definition in their own words, word/definition in the L1, and picture. Other substitutions include examples/non-examples or use in a sentence.

Formal definition	Definition in your own words
Word/definition in native language	Picture

How might you use, adapt or extend this in your classroom?

How will you group students for this activity?

What questions can you plan that will encourage critical thinking?

Table 4.20 Word Work Station!

Description: This is a compilation of quick vocabulary activities that students can create and engage in with limited or no teacher supervision or guidance.

Materials needed:

- Pencils, pens or markers
- Sticky notes
- Index cards
- Craft scissors (with different cuts)
- Jar
- Basket
- Paper

How to play:

Activity: Word Jar!

1. Place a word jar in the room.
2. Have students write down content words on strips of paper which they do not know the meaning of, they find interesting or they just want to learn more about. Collect the words and intersperse them into your daily instruction.

Activity: Vocabulary Puzzles!

1. Provide students with craft scissors *(with different cuts)*. Have them cut index cards in half, record a content word on one half and a corresponding definition or picture on the other half.
2. Students then shuffle the cards and match them back up.

Activity: Basket Bunch!

1. Teacher creates a basket of pictures, images and words related to the content area.
2. Students select cards from the basket and match them (cards either have a word, picture or definition, or students choose a card, say definition, match the word with the picture and explain why the picture represents that word).

(continued)

Table 4.20 continued

How might you use, adapt or extend this in your classroom?
How will you group students for this activity?
What questions can you plan that will encourage critical thinking?

Table 4.21 "Wordstorming"

Description: This activity is great for ELLs as it exposes them to the various forms of the vocabulary words, as well as providing examples illustrating the concept. It also provides them with opportunities for oral discourse and content extensions.

Materials needed:

- Pencils, pens or markers
- Cards with these three questions:

  - What are the other forms of this word?
  - Where might you expect to see or hear this word?
  - What synonyms or other words are related in meaning?

How to play:

1. Teacher introduces a content word.
2. Each group of students receives one of the three questions below:

   - What are the other forms of this word?
   - Where might you expect to see or hear this word?
   - What synonyms or other words are related in meaning?

3. Debrief as a group.

How might you use, adapt or extend this in your classroom?

How will you group students for this activity?
What questions can you plan that will encourage critical thinking?

Table 4.22 Write Around the Room!

Description: This is a great activity to use before structured writing. It provides students with opportunities to gather and select evidence to use in their writing. Students can be working with different texts depending on grouping and levels.
Materials needed:
• Pencils, pens or markers
• Text selections
• Paper
How to play:
1. Group students into pairs.
2. Have each group divide one piece of paper into eight equal sections.
3. In the top two sections, each pair writes two facts, examples, pictures or ideas relating to the content area, topic or theme (one in each section). They then pass their paper to another group, who add two more to the sheet, and so on.
4. Once the papers are completed, students compare and discuss the responses.
How might you use, adapt or extend this in your classroom?
How will you group students for this activity?
What questions can you plan that will encourage critical thinking?

Step 5: Examine Your Assessment Methods

Let's begin with the most important thing to know about grading: *Grades should not be reflective of language level.* Common pitfalls for content teachers include giving failing grades when students are unsuccessful with assessments, or inflating grades based solely on effort. Another common trap that classroom teachers fall into is providing too much assistance on tests and quizzes so that they basically do the work for the students. In both cases, grades are not reflective of students' true content knowledge. It is always important to consult with your administrator regarding your school/district's policy on grading.

Let's take some time to explore what this looks like in practice.

Here are four key questions to consider when determining grading practices for your ELLs:

1. *What are the students' language levels, and are any of them newcomers?* This question is important because assessments will need to be greatly modified in order to reduce language complexity.
2. *What modifications are you providing in your daily instruction?* This is important because there needs to be a *seamless match between instruction and assessment.* Teachers spend a great amount of time and effort on modifying their instruction to meet the varied needs and levels of ELLs in their classrooms. In order for students to meet with success on assessments, they need to be modified in a similar manner as the instruction. Non-modified versions of assessments limit student's ability to truly demonstrate what they know.
3. *What experiences have your students had with assessment formats?* A great starting point is to consider students' experiences *(or lack thereof)* with testing and assessment. What types of assessment formats have your students seen before? Take some time to research this information and provide your students with multiple opportunities to interact with different test formats *(both online and in print).* Even if you start with a few questions here and there for formative purposes, *repeated exposure is critical* to helping students gain confidence and reduce test anxiety. This will ensure that you are truly getting a gauge on what students know and are able to do.

    Here are some common assessment methods that may be new for your ELLs:

    ◆ Word problems
    ◆ Multiple choice
    ◆ Timed tests

◆ Fill in the blanks
◆ Online platforms used for state testing
◆ Other online formats that include the use of accessibility tools (ex.: drag and drop, highlighting, magnifier)
◆ Assessments that incorporate puzzles or humor

Be sure to collaborate with your ELL specialist to determine if a proposed assessment is appropriate, whether it needs to be modified and if grading needs to be differentiated.

4. *Is it easier to create a new assessment or modify the existing one?* Answers will vary depending on the language levels and content knowledge of your students. If you have newcomers, is it often less time consuming to create an assessment that mirrors instruction rather than to modify the one you already have. Either way, the most important thing to consider is the *importance of reducing language complexity* throughout. Take some time to review the linguistic challenges presented in Chapter 2, and edit your assessment accordingly.

See Table 4.23 for what reducing linguistic complexity looks like on an assessment item.

What was changed to modify this test item? First off, the *spacing of lines* was modified to accommodate for students' anticipated need to jot down the translation of certain words into their L1. Secondly, *key words* were underlined. Next, the *grammatical structure* of the item was changed from passive to active voice (*"one of the following items should be used" into "you should use"*). At the same time, some *unnecessary words were eliminated*. Lastly, *images were added* for answer choices. These simple changes made the question more accessible to linguistically diverse students.

When creating or modifying assessments for *newcomers*, consider the use of simple questions eliciting a true/false response, sometimes given orally. Assessment items should be accompanied with images whenever possible. Keep in mind that images for more complex and abstract ideas are often difficult to locate. If this is the case, use *associations*. Explain to your student that the images you are using are merely associations for the concept or a vocabulary word introduced. For example, to explain the word "sad," the teacher can utilize a serious of pictures demonstrating or evoking sad emotions. Be sure to use *several images* for association, so students can *identify the common theme* and have a better chance at comprehending the word meaning. When presented with just one image, ELLs may focus on an unimportant detail and misinterpret the meaning of the word introduced. Having students create their own association images after reading definitions of words or looking them up in a bilingual dictionary is another great idea. These student-created

Table 4.23

Original Assessment Item	Modified Assessment Item
You are heating a piece of glass for an experiment. In order to pick it up safely, one of the following items should be used: A. Paper towels B. Your hands C. Tongs	You are <u>heating</u> a piece of glass and need to <u>pick it up</u>. You should use: A. Paper towels B. Your hands C. Tongs

images can also be used in assessment. Students can be asked to match a series of pictures to the words or concepts.

Certain tests or parts of tests may also need to be eliminated altogether for newcomers, as they may be linguistically inappropriate. Let's take the concept of rhyming. Although it is a commonly assessed topic in English, some languages do not have many words that rhyme. Another good example is the use of nonsense words when teaching and assessing decoding skills. These can be especially challenging for students who are new to the language and are trying to attach meaning to them.

Cultural differences and bias should also be considered when creating and modifying assessments. Do the questions you are asking have cultural references? Do they ask for points of view? A few examples of this could be "count the items on a pizza," or "what would you do if there was a snow day?" Be sure to preview all your questions and eliminate cultural or regional references.

Reflection Questions

1. Imagine that you have several ELLs of varying levels in your classroom. What special considerations should be made when teaching and assessing these learners?
2. Examine the basic modification suggestions list provided in this chapter. Think about your current ELLs. Which modifications would be best for them and why?
3. Try one of the vocabulary activities provided in this chapter in your classroom. Reflect on how it went. What modifications did you make for struggling students and ELLs? What changes will you make to the activity when you use it next time?
4. Imagine that you are an administrator. What are some specific things you would expect the content teacher to do to support ELLs in their classroom? Create a "look fors" list.
5. What steps can you take to ensure that grading in your classroom is not a reflection of students' language levels?

5

How Is Math Unique?

Main Points

- ◆ Numbers and symbols do not have universal formation and interpretation.
- ◆ The way math problems are set up, presented and solved varies worldwide and can be confusing for ELLs.
- ◆ Preview math content and problems for cultural differences that may affect the answers.
- ◆ Be cognizant of words that have multiple meanings in math.
- ◆ Recording dates, telling time, using a new measurement system and showing work are just a few examples of the difficulties ELLs experience in math.

Getting Started

At one time or another, we have all heard the saying "math is a universal language." This stems from the thinking that numbers and operations are universal . . . *but are they*? If math is indeed universal, then even a student with linguistic barriers should meet with success when doing computation or word problems. This is not always the case; in fact, quite the opposite. Math is the outlier . . . the one content area that operates differently and can cause the greatest confusion for ELLs. If you teach math, there is no need to worry. In this chapter, we will explore these unique math differences and share best practices for addressing them.

Let's start with a short quiz! Solve these problems to the best of your ability.

1. $5.143 + 82 =$

2. $3\overline{)790,371}$

3. On 03/04/2008 Jack turned 5 years old. He went to Kindergarten in August of 2008. How old (to the month) was Jack when he started school?

4. Organize the following set of numbers into a <u>stem-and-leaf plot</u>: 56, 46, 61, 53, 41, 49.

Now let's examine these questions for potential *non-linguistic barriers*. When we look at questions 1 and 2 in the quiz, nothing seems to be problematic, right? If numbers are universal, an ELL should be successful at solving them as long as they understand the math content and the concepts. However, it's not as easy as it seems. Let's first take a look at the *number formation differences* below:

Figure 5.1

one	I	1 or 1
four	4 or 4	4
six	6	6
seven	7	7
nine	9	9

The *middle* column shows how we typically form numbers in the United States, and the *right* column shows numbers as they are formed in many countries in Eastern Europe, Africa, and some South American countries. To the adult eye, they don't look much different from each other when compared side by side. However, if you are a child and you have only seen 1's with horizontal lines at the bottom and 7's with a horizontal line through the middle, you are most likely going to be confused when you encounter the American style of writing these numerals.

Now let's take a look at 6's and 9's in the *right* column. The characteristic hooks used in forming these numbers in many countries make them look uniquely different from the traditionally formed 6's and 9's in the U.S. In addition, some numbers, the way they are formed in the U.S., may look like letters of the alphabet for students who come from non-Latin based writing systems. For example, the way a 6 is formed in the U.S. may look like a letter "ь" (soft sign) in Russian. So, your students may think there are variables and unknowns in problems represented by a letter. Consequently, they may not be able to solve such problems due to the misinterpretation of the number symbols.

Another big difference between math symbols in the U.S. and many other countries is the *opposite use of the decimal point (period) and a comma*. Table 5.1 shows the different ways decimals and thousands may be represented in different cultures.

As shown in the examples in Table 5.1, the use of periods and commas in math is reversed. In the U.S. system, periods indicate a separation of the whole number from its part (like in the example with two and one hundred five thousandths). Commas in the U.S. separate thousands and millions. However, in many other countries, these symbols have the reverse use which may cause misinterpretation and confusion.

Keeping this in mind, let's see why question 1 on the quiz may be misinterpreted. Depending on your interpretation of the period as a decimal

Table 5.1 Use of Decimal Points and Commas

U.S.	Other Countries
2.105 = two and one hundred five thousandths	2,105 = two and one hundred five thousandths
3,000,000 = three million	3.000.000 = three million
$4,000 = four thousand	$4.000 = four thousand

symbol versus a period separating thousands from hundreds, you may arrive at two different solutions:

5.143 + 82

```
   82            5.143
 + 5.143        +  82
 ───────        ───────
  87.143         5.225
```

When a math teacher assesses students' ability to line up numbers for addition according to their place value, he/she will most likely mark the problem on the *left* as correct and the problem on the *right* as incorrect. Imagine the confusion on a student's face when they get their papers back marked incorrectly. An ELL's language barrier will also most likely prevent him/her from explaining to the teacher how he/she got the answer. This may lead to the student becoming confused and disliking math. At the same time, the math teacher might get a false impression that the ELL is making the mistake illustrated above because he/she is not yet familiar with the concept of addition or lining up place values.

There is no way to know which system of representing decimals and thousands a student was taught ahead of time, but, knowing that the difference exists, throughout many countries in the world, will help teachers be more aware and analytical when looking at their newcomer's computation attempts.

Operation Signs

Math operation signs differ throughout the world. For example, the division sign formed this way /÷/ is often misinterpreted by ELLs who come from a system that uses a colon symbol /:/ for division.

The example above combines *number formation, use of a comma verses a period, and division operation sign* differences to illustrate how confusing a basic problem may appear to an ELL due to cultural differences.

Let's look at a student's reaction to the problem above. An ELL might look at the problem on the *left* and say that he/she does not know how to divide

Figure 5.2

U.S.	Eastern Europe, Africa, South America
$9.9 \div 3.3$	$9,9 : 3,3$

and subtract at the same time, as he/she may have only been exposed to /:/ representing division. Confusions like this happen often to newcomers. On top of that, language barriers may limit a student's ability to communicate their difficulties or confusions to the teacher. Consequently, a student's true level of performance in math might be skewed, which may result in poor grades or inappropriate placement in lower-leveled classes.

Differences in Setting up and Solving Problems

In many countries, *long division* is set up "backwards," or at least it looks that way to us in the U.S. The example in Figure 5.3 illustrates two ways of setting up the problem of dividing 3,726 into 36.

Figure 5.3

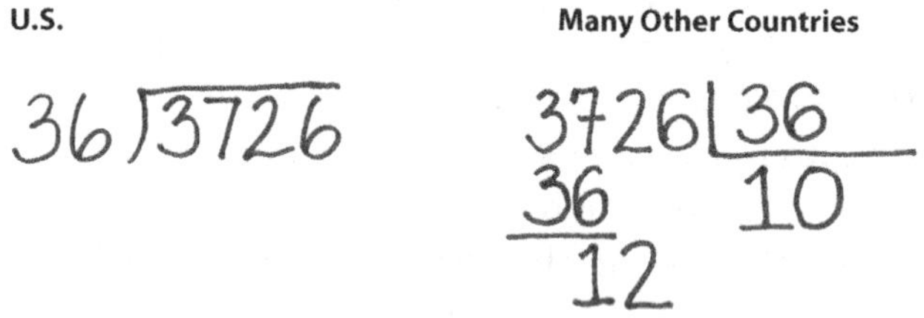

U.S.

$$36\overline{)3726}$$

Many Other Countries

$$3726\underline{\lfloor 36}$$
$$\underline{36} \quad 10$$
$$12$$

The way this division problem is set up on the *right* is completely different than how it would appear in the U.S. *(left)*. It is only partially completed in the example on the *right* with the purpose of demonstrating the first steps to solving it. The number being divided (dividend) is recorded first and then the number representing how many parts it is being divided into (divisor) is recorded second. The process of the actual solving looks a bit similar to what you are used to, but it is recorded under the dividend. The answer is recorded under the divisor. Let's examine question 2 on the quiz you took. An ELL could misinterpret it as dividing 3 into 790,371, since in his/her culture the number being divided is recorded first, and then the number to divide into is recorded second.

$$3\overline{)790,371}$$

However, if it were set up this way, an EL may be able to solve it:

$$790.371\,\big\backslash\,3$$

Long division is not the only example of a skill taught with a different procedure around the world. The traditional method of *adding and subtracting* two-, three-, four- or more digit numbers vertically starting from the right and finishing on the left is also not universal.

Figure 5.4

U.S. Traditional Method (right to left)	Other Method (left to right)

$$
\begin{array}{r}
\overset{2}{}\overset{\mathbf{5}}{\cancel{8}}\overset{1}{\cancel{6}}2 \\
-\,194 \\
\hline
168
\end{array}
$$

$$
\begin{array}{r}
\overset{1}{3}6\overset{1}{2} \\
-\,194 \\
\hline
2 \\
-\,17 \\
-18 \\
\hline
168
\end{array}
$$

There are methods where the process of adding and subtracting is started from the left. When math teachers see a student attempt to solve a problem that way, they may automatically think a student does not know the concept or is not using the procedure correctly.

See Figure 5.4 for differences between subtraction and addition procedures.

As seen in Figure 5.4 *(right-hand side)*, the problem solving procedure starts from the left side. The vertically aligned numbers on the left (hundreds) are subtracted. $3 - 1 = 2$ is recorded first. Then an attempt is made to subtract the next set of numbers (tens): $6 - 9$. Borrowing is needed. However, instead of borrowing from the top as is traditionally done in the U.S., the student borrows from the answer "2" in the hundreds column. The borrowing is recorded as $2 - 1$. Then $16 - 9 = 7$ is performed. The answer for the tens is recorded (7). The borrowing is repeated for the numbers on the right (ones): $12 - 4$ by recording $7 - 1$ in the tens' column. The final answer is calculated under the second horizontal line.

Confused yet? Most likely the answer is yes. Most people reading this probably got confused somewhere between lines two and three of the explanation. Now imagine how an ELL with low English proficiency would feel when presented with a similar explanation of "our" right-to-left method of adding or subtracting with borrowing, especially if he/she is used to solving it in a different way.

Figure 5.5 gives an example of addition with regrouping done in both a traditional right-to-left way (U.S.) and also a left-to-right method (many other countries).

Keep in mind . . . it is always easier to teach a skill to someone who does not know anything about the concept rather than to reteach someone who has a different idea or a way of doing it. So, if ELLs are not familiar with the math concepts you are using, the learning process will be easier. However, if they come with strong math skills and use different strategies or processes to get their answers,

Figure 5.5

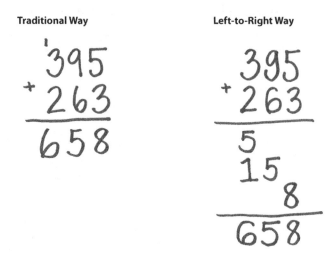

Traditional Way   Left-to-Right Way

take the time to understand the differences, validate these differences in problem solving and provide additional time and support as the student is relearning. Accepting and expressing interest in the way ELLs approach math differently will contribute to students feeling accepted and comfortable in your classroom.

Writing Dates and Time

Let's move on to discuss question 3 from the quiz. Here it is again:

On 03/04/2008 Jack turned 5 years old. He went to Kindergarten in August of 2008. How old (to the month) was Jack when he started school?

Aside from linguistic difficulties, what information can be confusing in this problem? How did you interpret 03/04/2008? As March 4th or April 3rd? That depends on where you come from. Many countries record *dates* from smallest to largest (date, month, year), which is different from the American approach (month, date, year). In the case of the problem above, the answers are different depending on how the date is interpreted. One of the most common confusions with dates often occurs before students even enter your classroom. If a student registers without an interpreter, and documents are presented in other languages, errors in birthdate interpretation can result in incorrect grade level placement. Check your student's birth certificates to be sure.

Time of day in the U.S. (using a 12-hour system with A.M. and P.M.) is also a point of confusion. Many countries use a 24-hour clock (often referred to as military time). Imagine the confusion that a 6:00 conference appointment notice could create for an ELL family. A parent who uses the 24-hour clock could assume it was an early morning meeting. So, instead of sending a note like this one *"Your parent conference is scheduled for 04/03 at 6 P.M.,"* consider writing it this way: *"Your parent conference is scheduled for April 3rd at 6 o'clock in the evening."* A small change like this can aid ELL families in comprehending your message.

Polysemous and Confusing Math Terms

Finally, let's examine question 4 from the quiz:

Organize the following set of numbers into a <u>stem-and-leaf plot</u>: 56, 46, 61, 53, 41, 49.

Without a doubt, if an ELL reading this problem tries to look up "stem-and-leaf plot" in their bilingual dictionary, what they are going to find is not helpful, unless he/she is using a dictionary specifically for math terms. This takes us back to the topic of *polysemous words* that are used in all content areas. In this case, stem and leaf is referring to the tens (stem) and ones (leaf) of recording data:

```
4 | 1,6,9
5 | 3,6
6 | 1
```
not at all something like this:

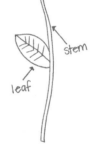

When such terms like "stem-and-leaf plot" or "box-and-whisker plot" are used in a math class, the teacher should also point out the literal meanings as well in order to contrast them. Adding polysemous terms to a word wall with two different meanings pictured underneath would also be very helpful. Be sure to always preview your materials for polysemous terms and plan accordingly.

Here are some additional polysemous math terms:

> face, cone, foot, yard, box, triangle, pi, root, square, table, log, significant, absolute, formula, mode, meter, edge, side, compass, star, diamond, count, function, integral, fraction, some/sum, difference, rational, manipulative, fair, balance, median, mean, chance, take away, times, into, from, tree, factor, evaluate, one/won, set, range, product, to/two/too, prime, odd, even, common

Cultural Differences in Math Problems

Try solving this *word problem*:

A school's **YBC** gets a large *fengi podatok* and uses it to improve the *plomaska*. Then the school students raise more funds and give the **YBC** $5,000, which is twice as much as the original *fengi podatok* was. How much money total did the school **YBC** get from both the *fengi podatok* and the students' fund raising? If each piece of *kachechi* costs $500, how many pieces of *kachechi* will they be able to buy for the *plomaska*?

Now replace *YBC* with **PTO**, *fengi podatok* with **monetary donation**, *plomaska* with **playground**, and *kachechi* with **equipment**. It makes sense now because culturally, we are familiar with what a PTO does, what monetary donations are, and types of playground equipment. It would not make any sense to an ELL if the things mentioned above are unfamiliar or do not exist in his/her culture.

Even though the computation involved in this word problem was quite simple, being stuck on unfamiliar words and concepts may have prevented you from clearly picturing the situation. In order to successfully solve math problems, students need to not only be familiar with the computation concepts involved, but also be able to clearly picture the situation described in order to decide which math concepts and operations to use.

Cultural information presented in word problems can also pose challenges for ELLs. Below is a list of just a few cultural terms used in math word problems that can be confusing to ELLs:

- ◆ Foods like pizza, pie, or other regional dishes *(when teaching fractions)*
- ◆ Information about sewing, measuring fabric, making curtains, quilting
- ◆ Snow accumulation
- ◆ U.S. city and state names, names of famous historical figures or events
- ◆ Holidays and traditions associated with them
- ◆ Birthday cake and candles
- ◆ Test grades and percentages associated with them *(used in algebra to teach mean, median, mode)*
- ◆ Money system *(coin values, heads/tails)*
- ◆ Clocks and telling time *(12-hour versus 24-hour clock)*
- ◆ Eating in a restaurant
- ◆ Calculating tax for a purchase
- ◆ Car value depreciation
- ◆ Store discounts, sales, and clearance events

This is by no means a complete list of cultural items that may be confusing to ELLs. These problems aren't impossible for ELLs to solve, but they require a mini background lesson or a demonstration, whenever possible, to introduce the students to concepts so that they can visualize each situation. Encountering problems like these allows for great teachable moments and gives content teachers the opportunity to teach math and American culture at the same time.

There are several best practices to consider when teaching math. Start with assigning a smaller number of problems testing the same math skill, as ELLs will require additional response time. Collaborating with your ELL specialist is essential. Take the time to preview instructional materials, tests and quizzes for cultural bias or linguistic challenges.

Money and Measurement System

Teaching *money* (especially coins), is an essential piece of the elementary math curriculum. For ELLs, money can prove to be a very difficult topic. U.S. coins (unlike many other countries) do not have their value written out in numbers on either side of the coin. Our coins say "dime," "nickel," "five cents," "quarter," "one cent," but nowhere can you locate the number representing the value of each coin (except for the gold dollars). Additionally, coin value is not universal throughout the world. Your ELL may come from a country where coins come in completely different denominations and values. Students may assume that an American coin that looks similar to a coin from their country in color or size has the same value. Another confusing part about American coins is that a dime is smaller than a nickel, but is worth more. Many students have a hard time with that, especially if they come from a country where the bigger the size of a coin is, the more it is worth. Lastly, there are U.S. state quarters in circulation. A strategy ELLs use is to memorize the pictures on the coins in order to recognize their value, but that does not work in the case of the U.S. quarters.

The best teaching advice for money and coins is to use real money instead of the plastic play money or the paper cut-outs for all instruction, games, practice, and even assessments. Handling real coins adds the element of seeing and feeling the actual coin with its color and weight, which is very helpful to all students, not just ELLs.

Next let's discuss the *measurement system* differences and issues associated with measuring distance, volume, temperature, etc. Many countries of the world use the metric system while in the U.S. the customary system is used. It does not take students long to notice that the rulers in their new math classrooms look different and have both inch and centimeter marks. So, when ELLs are introduced to words like inches, feet, yards, and miles, some students tend to initially assume that these are just different words for what they know as centimeters, meters, kilometers, etc. They do not realize and are often confused by the customary conversion, as it is much more complicated to convert inches to feet, for example, because it does not use the intervals of 10's system that the metric system uses.

Metric System:
1 cm = 10 mm
1 dm = 10 cm
1 m = 100 cm
1 km = 1,000 m

Customary System:
1 ft = 12 in
1 yard = 3 ft
1 mi = 5280 ft
1 mi = 1760 yards

Difficult to compare, isn't it? Many students struggle with the measurement system, and "easy" problems such as *"Which is the best unit to use for measuring the distance between Pittsburgh and Gettysburg: inches, yards, feet, or miles?"* become very complicated as the students first need to determine what "Pittsburgh" and "Gettysburg" are (people, schools, or cities), and then decide which unit is best to use to measure the distance between them.

Consider this temperature related problem:

Is it hot or cold outside when the temperature is 32°? What would you wear in such weather?

ELLs who come from countries that use Celsius might say it was a hot day and they could wear shorts and t-shirts, as opposed to the expected

Table 5.2 Conversion Table

Degrees Fahrenheit °F	Degrees Celsius °C	Notes
212	100	water boils
100	37.8	
90	32.2	
70	21.1	average room temperature
50	10	
32	0	water freezes
0	−17.8	

response of winter attire. This example illustrates how confusing the use of Celsius vs. Fahrenheit can be to ELLs. Since the conversion formula is not an easy one to use (Celsius to Fahrenheit – multiply degrees Celsius by 9, divide by 5, add 32), we recommend using a table similar to Table 5.2 that a student could access when needed.

Technology

In math and science classes students are expected to use *technology*. Sometimes ELLs come from schools where access to technology is limited or non-existent. Schools in many countries do not have designated funding to purchase any instructional materials outside of textbooks, paper and pencils. In some cases, the reasons for lack of technology usage may be different. Some countries do not introduce the use of calculators because students are expected to do computation in their heads or find the answer using a pencil and paper method only. In such countries, calculators are not introduced until students are enrolled in more advanced math courses. Consider these differences when planning instructional activities and lessons that involve the use of any type of technology, from computers to calculators. For example, in secondary classrooms, graphing calculators are a big part of math instruction and assessment. Newcomer ELLs often get overwhelmed by fast-paced explanations of how to use graphing calculators to solve more complex problems. Taking the time to explicitly teach calculator functions is critical. It is also helpful to provide students with numbered steps and pictures of the calculator buttons as a reference.

Showing Their Work

In the U.S., we expect students to *show their work* when solving math problems. In many countries, students are taught just the opposite . . . not to show their work, which can be considered a sign of weakness. Often times, ELLs initially refuse to show their work, as they may come from a country where mental math and rote memorization are the norm. If you notice your ELL is doing this, it is important to have a conversation with him/her in order to explain why showing their work is not considered a weakness, but rather an expectation. Take the time to demonstrate how problems are graded, and explain that points can still be awarded for showing work even if the final answer is incorrect. Seeing how students solve problems can help to identify misunderstandings or non-universal computation differences.

Curricular Differences

As with many subject areas, there are *curricular differences* in math across the world. When working with ELLs, assumptions can't be made relative to concepts and skills that have been taught and mastered at certain grade levels. Identifying a student's missing skills takes time. Most likely, these gaps will reveal themselves during your instruction. If you do notice any gaps, be sure to share this information with your ELL specialist and collaborate on ways to address them.

Other Difficulties ELLs May Encounter in the Math Classroom

Working in *collaborative groups* is a common practice and expectation in the American classroom, but is not common in many countries. If your ELLs have never experienced working with partners before, they may interpret this to be unstructured free time or recess which may result in confusion and behavioral issues. It is also important to note that in some cases, ELLs may come from societies where male and female students are not grouped together for instructional purposes. Consequently, an ELL may experience discomfort being placed in a collaborative group with a partner of the opposite gender. It is important to be sensitive and understanding in the beginning, but with time, the students will need to adjust to their new environment where male and female students work alongside each other and are treated equally.

Another confusing concept to ELLs, and sometimes even their families, is the **use of manipulatives** in the classroom. Elementary math classrooms are full of blocks, counting bears, dice, and other bright and colorful instructional materials. To the unaccustomed eye, these may look like toys, which can cause distraction and confusion as to why they are being used for instruction. Imagine the look on your face if a parent approached you and made the comment that your classroom was too distracting with all the "toys" around, and that he/she would prefer if more time was spent on instruction with paper and pencils. Take some time to explain to ELL parents how and why manipulatives are being used in your classroom. If parents are unable to see this in action, consider sending home photos of their child using them as instructional tools. This will help them to understand the role that manipulatives play in math.

Worksheets that double as puzzles can also cause confusion for ELLs. Once all the problems are completed correctly, a joke is revealed. These jokes are most often built on word play, allusions, homonyms or idiomatic expressions. Here are just a few examples:

Q: *Why did the time seem to go so quickly at the glue factory?*
A: *It was fast paste.*
Q: *Why did the dog have to go to court?*
A: *It got a barking ticket.*

Newcomer ELLs spend a lot of time trying to understand first how to solve the problems then how to interpret the joke. Students can get discouraged that they are the only ones in class who can't pick up on the humor. This does not mean such worksheets should be avoided, but consider assigning an alternate worksheet devoid of linguistic challenges.

Strategies to Use When Teaching ELLs

◆ Rewrite word problems in simple English, using short sentences, pictures, known symbols, and other illustrations that provide meaning.
◆ Teach words that are associated with each of the operations and comparison words necessary for understanding quantitative relationships (see Table 5.3 that students can create and use as a resource).
◆ Help students prepare a card file of number words and their symbols.
◆ Encourage the use of diagrams and drawings to show relationships.
◆ Help students prepare a glossary of mathematical terms.
◆ Give the special mathematical meanings for common polysemous terms (table, face, leg, etc.).

Table 5.3 Math Operations Vocabulary

+	−	÷	×	=
add plus and combine	subtract minus less take away	divide divided by over into	multiply times by as a factor	equals result answer in total

>	≥	<	≤

- ◆ Limit the number of problems a student needs to solve to represent an essential mathematical concept.
- ◆ Allow extra time to complete classwork assignments.
- ◆ Encourage students to use bilingual and standard dictionaries.
- ◆ Use paper folds for note-taking.
- ◆ Make a variety of math manipulatives and objects available in the classroom.
- ◆ Incorporate hands-on, cooperative learning activities based on real-life situations.
- ◆ Use alternative and formative assessment methods (observations, checklists, student's self-appraisals, rubrics).
- ◆ Collaborate with the ELL specialist in your school to modify instruction and determine appropriate accommodations.

Reflection Questions

1. In your experience working with ELLs, have you encountered a student who formed their numbers, symbols or operation signs differently, or was confused by some of the symbols or processes used in math in the U.S.? How did you (or would you) approach this situation?
2. Describe your attempts to understand the long division problem, or left-to-right vertical addition and subtraction problems used in this chapter. How might ELLs feel when they are introduced to our methods of solving such problems, and what are some strategies you can use to address this?
3. Examine math word problems you use in your classroom for cultural information that may be confusing to ELLs. How can you introduce the necessary background information so that all students are able to understand these problems?
4. Let's take word problems one step further. Practice reducing the linguistic complexity in an upcoming word problem from your curriculum (rewrite in simple present tense, remove extraneous information and cultural references).
5. Think about an upcoming chapter or unit of study. What terms are polysemous or may be confusing to ELLs? How might you address these potential misunderstandings?

6

What Are the Most Effective Ways to Collaborate with ELL Staff?

Main Points

- Regular and meaningful communication with your ELL specialist is key.
- Be cognizant of each other's schedules and remain as flexible and accommodating as possible.
- Remember to communicate schedule changes with each other.
- Discussions should include big ticket items such as curriculum and lesson plan sharing, resource sharing, modifications, accommodations and grading.
- Student snapshots should be shared regularly with each other and maintained to show progress over time.
- Be sure to include the ELL specialist in all meetings and grade-level discussions/co-planning opportunities.
- Save time and streamline support by sharing copies of your materials, answer keys and resources with your ELL specialist.
- Co-teaching with an ELL specialist can benefit all students.

Getting Started

Whether you have one ELL in your classroom or many, it is important to establish a *collaborative working relationship* with your ELL specialist as soon as possible. Take the time to learn who it is, how often he/she is in your school and what professional development and instructional supports are available to you and your ELLs.

There are three key steps to consider when working with your ELL specialist:

Step 1: Conduct an initial meeting and share key information.

Step 2: Develop an effective communication plan.

Step 3: Establish a plan for instruction and assessment.

Step 1: Conduct an Initial Meeting and Share Key Information

As teachers, we know how precious and limited time is during the school day. Once you know who the ELL specialist is in your school, set up a time to *meet one on one*. During this initial meeting, key pieces of information should be shared and discussed. Take some time to jot down questions you have for the ELL specialist and information you would like to share or receive.

At the initial meeting with your ELL specialist, establish how frequently you will meet in person, and what the *expectations are for maintaining regular communication* with one another. Be sure to spend your energy and focus on establishing good communication with one another and value each other's time. Remember, most problems can be avoided with regular communication. Stay connected with each other and you can avoid misunderstandings and challenges when working together to support your ELLs. Establish a communication plan that will pave the way for regular exchanges of information throughout the year.

Other important information to obtain at your initial meeting is a copy of the student's official ELL accommodation document, as well as the ELL service plan (if one exists). It is important to know that ELL accommodations carry the same legal weight as IEP accommodations. Be sure to also consult with your school test coordinator to ensure that you are in compliance. Tables 6.1 and 6.2 will provide you with starting points of important items to consider and templates that can be used to exchange student specific information.

Familiarize Yourself With Different ELL Service Models

Different ELL service models exist in schools throughout the U.S. The most common ones are pull-out, plug-in *(sometimes also referred to as push-in)* and sheltered instruction. Communicate with your ELL specialist to determine which model(s) of instruction your school/district follows, and which would be most appropriate for your ELLs.

Table 6.1 Initial Meeting Checklist/Discussion Items

Initial meeting date:	
Key information to discuss/share:	**Notes:**
Email/phone (content teacher): Email/phone (ELL specialist):	
Classroom teacher schedule/support needs:	
ELL specialist schedule/possible service/support times:	
Name(s)/level(s)/languages of ELLs (and does the family need an interpreter):	
Name(s) of students who have recently exited from or did not qualify for ELL services (and does the family need an interpreter):	
Name(s) of students with IEPs, 504s, medical issues/concerns, and/or those being referred for additional support services:	
Special classroom/grade-level circumstances to consider:	
Dates/days/times of grade-level team and pacing meetings and other related meetings (ELL specialist should be invited/present):	
Professional development/co-planning opportunities and access to supplemental resources:	

Table 6.2 ELL Instructional Snapshot

Note: See also Table 7.1 for an ELL Linguistic Snapshot

Student name/grade/birthdate:
Native language/length of time in U.S.:
Special considerations about student's background (culture, trauma, literacy in L1, prior schooling, etc.):
English proficiency level: Reading: Listening: Speaking: Writing:
Current instructional levels/recent test scores (math, reading):
Student's schedule/teachers:
Additional interventions student is receiving:
State testing status/exemptions:
Accommodations (must receive for testing and daily instruction; also be sure to receive an official signed copy from the ELL specialist for your records):

Daily modification/scaffolding supports:
Big instructional goals/expected progress and timelines:
Other information: (student's strengths, interests and motivations):

Pull-out is usually a one-on-one or small group time during which students work on improving their English language skills in speaking, listening, reading and writing. During pull-out sessions, an ELL specialist is able to address individual linguistic needs of ELLs. Ideally, language and grade-level content should be paired in order to ensure alignment and access once school survival vocabulary and phrases are established.

Plug-in (push-in) is a service model during which an ELL specialist provides support in the mainstream classroom where ELLs are placed together with their monolingual peers. The ELL specialist can either co-teach an activity or part of a lesson or simply support ELLs by modifying or scaffolding instruction, assessments or certain assignments. The level and depth of the support should be based on the student's English proficiency and their ability to access the curriculum.

Note: During both pull-out and plug-in service models, ELLs are placed in the mainstream classroom with their native English speaking peers.

Sheltered instruction looks different, however. Students are taught by content and ELL specialists at the same time and ELLs are grouped together with each other for instruction. The grade-level material is adapted linguistically to meet the students' language needs. For example, instead of presenting new material through lectures or reading of complex extended texts, students are specifically instructed in key vocabulary and the content is presented in a less "linguistically heavy" way, avoiding idioms, passive tense or lengthy sentence structures. This model of instruction is often seen in school districts with high ELL populations.

There are various opinions and discussions around which model is best to follow instructionally and/or fiscally, and the truth is there are benefits and drawbacks for each of them. No matter which model is used in your district, there is one important point to be made about effective instruction of ELLs: content and language instruction must go hand in hand. Students need to improve their language skills in order to gain better understanding of content instruction, and at the same time their language instruction needs to be delivered through content to help students make more sense of the material, increase the frequency of key vocabulary exposure and the use of necessary language structures.

Step 2: Develop an Effective Communication Plan

In order to deliver cohesive content and language instruction that best supports ELLs, *regular and meaningful* communication is necessary between you and the ELL specialist. Ideally, you should meet weekly to discuss upcoming units of study, assignments and assessments, along with schedule changes and other issues that may arise. Instructional goals should also be discussed and *content/language goals* should be paired and planned out on a weekly basis. Modifications, accommodations (request a copy of the accommodation form), and grading should also be regular topics of discussion. It is also important for the ELL specialist to be invited to team or pacing meetings, grade-level co-planning sessions and discussions about data. Ideally, the ELL specialist's job should be balanced between working with students and supporting content teachers, making connections in the school and developing and delivering professional development on demand.

As a classroom teacher, you are responsible for teaching content lessons and units of study in a specific sequence. This can create challenges for your ELLs if they have linguistic barriers or lack of prior knowledge necessary to understand the lessons. By *sharing your lesson plans* with the ELL specialist, you can get suggestions on how to scaffold or alter certain parts to ensure accessibility. He/she can also support the students by previewing your texts, going over assignments and reviewing quizzes and tests.

Key considerations for collaborating with your ELL specialist and supporting your ELLs:

- ◆ **Meet regularly** *(weekly or bi-weekly, depending on individual student/ content area)* to discuss student progress, assignments, grading and modification needs, as well as any schedule changes.
- ◆ Provide him/her with a copy of all *classroom texts, handouts, projects, directions, worksheets, quizzes and tests* in advance and *work collaboratively* to *modify* them.

- Consider *alternative assignments* whenever appropriate (*ex: reduced number of questions, condensed writing assignments, etc.*).
- Discuss acceptable *assignment lengths and requirements*.
- Send updated *assessment info* for tracking student progress.
- Seat the student in an *easily accessible location* so targeted support can be provided.
- Allow the student *extra time* for assignments and assessments.

Consider using a communication template that you can exchange with the ELL specialist on a weekly basis. Table 6.3 captures key academic information that will guide your instruction and conversations with one another.

Table 6.3 ELL Specialist/Content Teacher Weekly Communication Template

This week's schedule changes *(content teacher)*:	This week's schedule changes *(ELL specialist)*:
This week's content objectives *(content teacher)*:	This week's language objectives *(ELL specialist)*:
Key vocabulary by subject area *(content teacher)*:	
Upcoming projects/assignments *(content teacher)*:	Suggested modifications *(from ELL specialist)*:
How will the student(s) be assessed?	

(continued)

Table 6.3 continued

What progress do we expect to see?
Missing/late work: *(Is it feasible or reasonable for the student to complete? Will they need direct instructional support to finish?)*
How can the ELL specialist help you this week? *(Resources, support for a specific day/lesson?)*

Anticipated challenges, concerns and special considerations *(content teacher)*:	Anticipated challenges, concerns and special considerations *(ELL specialist)*:

Other:

Communicating and Collaborating with Your Administrators

Now that you have developed a plan for regular and meaningful communication with your ELL specialist, it is time to share this plan with your school administrators. Set up a time for you and the ELL specialist to meet with the administration team to share *students' successes and challenges*. Bring work samples and test scores that show progress and achievement over time, along with details about how you are working together to best support your ELLs. Invite administrators into your classroom and encourage your ELLs to build relationships with them. They can also provide you with valuable insight about strengthening instruction, along with ideas for parent outreach and available community resources. They may even call upon you both to provide professional development and support for other school staff! Some ideas for ELL workshops you could offer may include: top four things to know about your ELLs, strategies for modifying content and assessments, collaboration practices and exploring the impact of culture and language on learning.

Step 3: Establish a Plan for Instruction and Assessment

Once you and the ELL specialist have agreed upon a communication plan, the next step is to discuss how he/she will be supporting you both *in the classroom and beyond*. One of the most important things to keep in mind is that each of you is an expert in your area. You are the master of content, and he/she will know the ins and outs of language acquisition. You will need to trust each other's expertise to merge content and language instruction for your ELLs. The ELL specialist will most likely rely on your expertise to make sure he/she understands the material, as it is impossible to be an expert in all subject areas. Take the time to explain challenging concepts and provide him/her with notes, answer keys and copies of your handouts. Also be sure to provide him/her with access to online resources, district curriculum and any changes/additions you have made.

ELL specialists need to be able to *preview content* to be delivered in the classrooms. Looking over the materials and assessments helps the ELL specialist to effectively prepare students for success in the classroom. Language and content objectives should be set for every lesson. For example, an ELL's linguistic objective may be adding "–ed" to verbs to form regular past simple tense (*look – looked, serve – served, protest – protested, etc.*). This language objective can be achieved through social studies content, like the Civil Rights Movement, by actively reading and discussing an appropriately leveled text on the topic and highlighting regular past tense verbs. Another example could be teaching comparative structures like "greater than" or "less than" through math content and solving inequalities similar to this one: "A number increased by 2 is greater than 7". Language needs to be taught and practiced through the grade level content.

Co-Teaching: Try It!

This may be a new and challenging concept for both of you, but plug-in (push-in) can prove to be quite effective when you each share equal roles in the classroom. Encourage and empower the ELL specialist to support all students to the extent possible, rather than hovering over one or two ELLs exclusively. This involves *dedicated co-planning time*. Consider starting with the ELL specialist leading a vocabulary game, review activity, an introduction into a new unit or topic or an exploration or engagement activity. All students can benefit from a change of pace, method and personality of the teacher and mode of instruction. It is also a confidence booster for your ELLs, as they will not feel singled out as needing individualized support.

Reflection Questions

1. What ELL service model does your school follow and how is it determined which support students receive?

2. Modify or create a communication template that would work for you to exchange information with your ELL specialist. What key items are most important to share with each other?

3. Think ahead to your next unit of study. What materials, handouts, content and answer keys will you need to provide to your ELL specialist in advance? Which one(s) may need to be modified?

4. What type of professional development would your colleagues benefit from the most? Collaborate with your ELL specialist and brainstorm a list that you can share with your administrators. Find out what opportunities might be available to you at the district level.

5. Schedule a time for peer observations (ELL specialist and another content teacher). Debrief best practices with one another and plan next steps for enhancing your instruction.

7

What Should I Do if I Suspect There Is a Learning Disability?

Main Points

- ◆ Collaboration with your ELL specialist and other colleagues is key in this process.
- ◆ Start with gathering and documenting key information relative to the student's journey towards achieving English language proficiency, and examine progress.
- ◆ Research background information about the student (academic, medical).
- ◆ Attempt and document a variety of supports and interventions.
- ◆ Take anecdotal notes and share them with the team.
- ◆ Compile all your documentation and work with your colleagues to determine next steps.
- ◆ Be sure to consider and adhere to school-specific procedures for referring to special education.

Getting Started

Determining whether or not an ELL has a learning disability can be a daunting and seemingly impossible task. Often times, learning disabilities and language differences will present in similar ways and, without a strong process or a team of educators who are trained in navigating the process, misidentification or over-identification can occur. Information gathering is essential. Generally, the more information you discover, the more questions you may have.

Before considering making a referral to special education, there are *five key steps* you can follow that will help you better navigate this process:

> **Step 1: Connect with your ELL specialist.**
>
> **Step 2: Explore the student's second language learning progress.**
>
> **Step 3: Research and gather background information about the student.**
>
> **Step 4: Observe and document!**
>
> **Step 5: Collaborate with colleagues and determine your next steps.**

Step 1: Connect With Your ELL Specialist

It seems obvious, but the first step in this process should be connecting with the ELL specialist in your building. Find out if he/she also shares your concerns, and what other information they have about the student. Often times, they were present or may have even assisted during the student's registration. Most likely, he/she has information that may help to provide additional insight into the student's background, culture and other relevant information. In addition, they most likely work with school interpreters and translators on a regular basis, and may be able to track down additional information or help to get answers to questions that may arise. Start the process together, communicate often and develop a plan for next steps.

Step 2: Explore the Student's Second Language Learning Progress

The next step in the process is to step back and get the "big picture" of the student's language learning. Work collaboratively with the ELL specialist to put together an ELL snapshot *(see Table 7.1)* that captures key information you will need as you examine his/her linguistic background and classroom modifications and accommodations. Having this information all in one place will help to paint a clear picture of this student for others who will be part of this process.

Table 7.1 ELL Linguistic Snapshot

Note: See also Table 6.2 for an ELL Instructional Snapshot.

Student name:	**School/grade:**
Date of birth:	**Native language:**
Country of birth:	**U.S. entry date:**
ELL level:	**Length of time in ELL program:**
ELL testing history/scores:	
Classroom modifications:	
Current testing accommodations:	
Trauma and/or special considerations:	

It is important to note that there are many factors that may influence a person's ability to learn a second language. These should be considered when looking at the whole child. Factors include, but are not limited to:

◆ Education and literacy (in L1 and L2)
◆ Instructional program(s)
◆ Family/school/community support
◆ Cultural background/differences
◆ Culture shock
◆ Personality/learning style

- ◆ Interest in school
- ◆ Attitudes towards learning a new language
- ◆ Trauma/home life

How will you know there is a problem? Here are some red flags to consider:

- ◆ You notice peculiar behavior
- ◆ Teammates come to you with concerns
- ◆ Child is not progressing in any area at the rate you feel is appropriate for his/her circumstances
- ◆ Administrators or teachers discuss retention
- ◆ Child has been retained and is still not catching up to appropriate grade level expectations (assuming not language related)
- ◆ Child has been in the ESOL program several years and isn't showing progress *(Put all the ELL language tests side by side. Do you notice any areas of regression?)*

Step 3: Research and Gather Background Information About the Student

Knowing information about your students is key to providing the best education possible. The information gathering process can be especially challenging for many different reasons. Sometimes records simply don't exist or were left behind when families moved. The student's educational and medical histories should be considered and explored (see Tables 7.2 and 7.3). An interpreter may be needed to communicate with the family. It is important

Table 7.2 Educational History Checklist

Student name: School/grade: Date:		
Key school information to explore	Questions to consider	Details/notes/important dates
If school occurred outside the U.S., how did it work?	Length/months of school year; was there compulsory attendance; were students separated by grade/age/ ability; was the student "tracked" to a certain career path and why *(this may also provide some insight about student's academic ability)*	

What were the prior schooling experience(s)?	What are the years, grades, languages and experiences of the student's prior formal schooling?	
How does the student feel about school?	Is he/she motivated to learn in a new environment? Is it the parents' motivation that drives schooling? Does the student complete his/her homework on their own?	
Has there been interrupted schooling?	Yes/no; location; circumstances	
Are there attendance issues?	Is there a history of frequent absences? Why?	
Was the student retained?	If yes, what grade(s)? Why? (If retention occurred outside the U.S., did the student receive any additional academic services and why?)	
Did the student have an IEP or comparable identification/ services from the previous school?	If yes, obtain a recent copy. What was the identified disability and how did officials arrive at that diagnosis? What language(s) were used for testing and why?	
Has the student worked with a specialist in the previous school?	If yes, what type(s) of services did the student receive? How often?	
Other		

Table 7.3 Medical History Checklist

Student name: School/grade: Date:		
Key school information to explore	Questions to consider	Details/notes/ important dates
Date/results of last hearing test	Where did test occur? Is there a history of ear infections?	
Date/results of last vision test	Does the student wear/ever worn glasses? Is there a history of vision issues?	
Date/results of last physical exam	Does the doctor have any concerns?	
Is there a family history of disabilities and/or difficulties with school?	Do parents/siblings face the same issues?	
Developmental milestone issues (age of first words/sentences, walking, etc.)	Is there a history of speech/language issues? How does the student compare to their siblings?	
History of childhood diseases, injuries or other health issues	At what age did these occur? What were the treatments, if any?	
Former/current medications	Is the student currently taking any medications (short or long term)?	
History of trauma, accidents, emotional issues	Were there any traumatic events that occurred in the student's life (physical, emotional or situational)?	
History of socialization/behavioral issues	Is the student able to make friends easily? What specific behavioral issues exist (if any)?	
Socialization concerns	How would you characterize the student's relationships with peers and family? Are there any concerns?	
Other extrinsic/intrinsic factors		
Other		

to note that parents/guardians may be reluctant to share personal and medical information. Be sure to consult with your school administration prior to beginning the research process, as there may be additional procedures and guidelines to consider. It is also good to make contact with other specialists in your building (math, reading, special education, etc.).

Step 4: Observe and Document!

As soon as you suspect there are learning issues present, begin to document your daily and weekly observations, along with instructional practices, successes and challenges. Documentation is critical and an extremely valuable step in the special education pre-referral process. It is important that each teacher who works with the student is also documenting their concerns, observations and practices. This will help to paint a clear picture of the student's strengths and areas of concern. Also, if everyone reflects and records teacher supports and professional practice, you can learn from each other and get new ideas for instruction and assessment.

It is important to note that students who are learning a second language may often exhibit behaviors that mirror those of a learning disability. Tables 7.4 and 7.5 outline checklists that target the most critical information that you should explore and gather. Remember to share this responsibility with your ELL specialist and be sure to keep detailed and concise notes.

Table 7.4 Teacher Support Checklist

Student name: School/grade: Date:	
Questions to consider	Details/notes/implementation dates
How are you differentiating content, process and assessment in order to ensure access?	
What materials of instruction are working well and why?	
What materials of instruction are not working well and why?	
What teaching and assessment methods work well and why?	

(continued)

Table 7.4 continued

What teaching and assessment methods are <u>not</u> working and why?	
How is this student able to show what he/she knows?	
What in-class or pull-out interventions are being offered?	
Other	

Table 7.5 Sample Behavioral Observation Tool

Student name: School/grade: Date:		
Behavior	Antecedent (if behavioral)	Observed (Y/N); frequency, date, circumstances
Difficulty remembering information (*short or long term*)		
Difficulty processing and/or retrieving information		
Work avoidance and/or shutdown		
Disorganization		
Defiance		
Hyperactivity		
Poor attention		
Other		

Step 5: Collaborate With Colleagues and Determine Your Next Steps

Review and Meet

Now that you have gathered information about the student's background, educational and medical history and classroom performance, it is time to

Table 7.6 Items to Bring to Student Meetings

Student name: School/grade: Date:	
Data/item(s)	Key information/notes:
ELL student file	
ELL learning plan	
Copies of ELL test score reports	
Assessment data from content areas of concern	
Intervention records, information	
Anecdotal notes	
Background information about the student *(educational history and medical checklists)*	
Work samples	
Recent meeting notes	
Other	

review your data and collaborate with your colleagues and the parents. Next steps may or may not involve a formal referral to special education. It really depends on what information has been gathered, what interventions are being met with success and what the team feels is the best course of action. Perhaps additional interventions may be most appropriate, or more time is needed to explore new ideas for modifications and accommodations. Start with a team meeting and be sure to invite the parent/guardian.

Important Considerations if Making a Referral to Special Education

If the team decides that a referral is the most appropriate next step, it is important to consult with your ELL specialist to see if additional testing needs to occur prior to the meeting. Often times, an ELL or dual language specialist will want to conduct dominant language testing prior to a special education screening meeting. This will help to inform which language(s) should be used for future testing. If the special education committee orders dual language testing (ex. cognitive, academic, speech/language, etc.), it is important to note that validity may be compromised when assessments are not published in target language. It is critical to work collaboratively with special education staff to develop a statement for the Individualized Education Plan (IEP).

Reflection Questions

1. What procedures do you have in your school for identifying ELLs for special education?
2. What percentage of your ELL population is dual identified (ELL/special education)? How does this compare to the overall special education population in your school?
3. What are the biggest challenges you have faced in identifying ELLs for special education?
4. What additional supports can you put in place in your classroom and deliver yourself? What interventions are available at your school?
5. You suspect one of your ELLs may also have some learning issues. What would be your actions prior to referring to special education?

Conclusion

Let's take a step back, review some of the main points from the book and think about where we go from here.

In Part I, we explored the importance of *getting to know your ELLs.* This begins with researching information about how students' backgrounds, native languages and cultures may impact their learning. How might you respond if they have experienced trauma? What if they have limited or interrupted schooling? What routines may they struggle with in your classroom? What are their English levels and when were they last assessed? What can you learn about their cultures? What is your plan for connecting with families? *These are just a few questions you will need to ask yourself as you begin to learn about your ELLs.*

We also explored how *linguistics impacts teaching and learning.* What is your plan for previewing your instructional materials for linguistic and cultural barriers? How are students' native languages structured and what similarities exist between English? What challenges will they experience as they learn content? *Examining your content through a linguistic lens is critical for your ELLs.*

In Part II, we examined *instructional practice.* Remember, ELLs should not be removed from the challenges set forth in the standards, but rather supported in meeting them. Always start with your *grade-level content* and go from there. Choose the essentials to be taught and plan accordingly. How are you making content accessible for your ELLs? Do you have high expectations for your learners and do they share the same expectations for themselves? How will you anticipate and plan for misunderstandings? Do your assessment methods match your instruction? What will you do if you suspect there are issues beyond language? *Ask yourself the hard questions and hold yourself accountable for answering them.*

Remember, the key to strengthening instructional practice is *collaboration.* Dedicate time to co-plan with your ELL specialist and other colleagues. Pair content and language objectives in daily instruction. Discuss student progress and set learning goals together. Embrace a growth mindset and be open to new ways of doing things. Find out what resources exist in your school and district. Share best practices and out-of-the-box ideas. *Regular collaboration and communication with each other will pave the way for student success.*

Enjoy the journey you are about to take with your ELLs and their families!

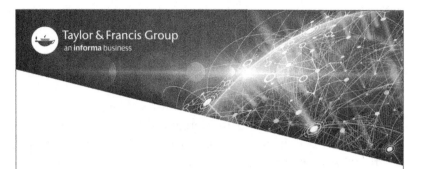

Made in United States
North Haven, CT
22 September 2023

41855753R00063